MINDLESS SELLING

BY DAVE KURLAN

1stBooks –rev. 3/23/01

DEDICATION

I dedicate this book to my wonderful wife Deborah Penta-Kurlan, who supported, encouraged, read, reread, edited, endorsed, and finally loved my work. If it weren't for her I would have never undertaken this project. Her inspiration, insight, incredible creativity, and desire to see my projects come to fruition whenever 1 became frustrated is appreciated.

TABLE OF CONTENTS

INTRODUCTION

1

"Your knowledge of selling as a process is not enough to help you to execute effectively on a daily basis."

Dave Kurlan

For the last twenty-two years I have carved a path in selling which consistently went in unusual directions. In 1973 I actually chose sales instead of accidentally falling into it like most people. I thought selling would teach me how to get along with the multitude of people with whom I found getting along terribly difficult. Most people accept a position in sales because it provides them with an opportunity to meet people. While most future salespeople are told they would be good at selling because of their outgoing personalities, knack for telling stories, cracking jokes, and holding people's attention, I was told flat out that I would fail because I never spoke to anyone. While other salespeople were making Sales, I was often just trying to make it through one more day. While others were using their charming personalities, ample enthusiasm, and abundance of confidence, I was just trying to develop some of all three.

Some things have a way of turning out really funny. For me it was succeeding at selling, despite my fears, my discomforts, my early lack of emotional maturity, and my lack of experience with other human beings. I was actually doing well after a couple of years and eventually found myself training, managing, and recruiting salespeople. I seemed to have a knack for management, but just as in the case with selling, I really didn't have a clue as to why. There was one thing that I was sure of in 1975. Not only did I want to remain in sales, but also I wanted to be a sales trainer. That was a pretty far-fetched goal for someone with my limited experience and tender age, but it proved to be prophetic.

My career training salespeople turned out to be as different as my career in sales. Once I mastered the process, I was able to effectively recreate it with consistency, and most importantly, I was helping others to do it as well. Despite my biggest weakness, which I imagined was my youth, but which turned out to be my inability to play politics, sales was my destiny. I carved a niche for myself in the training world that would differentiate me from the rest of the pack.

While the concept of evaluating salespeople wasn't a new one, I have a very unique approach: Evaluating salespeople prior to training, rather than the old practice of testing prior to hiring. I had already determined that while most psychological profiles were accurate in demonstrating the emotional make up of an individual, they did little to predict what would actually happen to that individual in varied selling situations. They didn't explain the reasons for those outcomes and failed to provide direction to correct particular problems. They often demonstrated an "either/or" loophole. For instance, if an individual has good, warm, nurturing people skills, then those tests were designed to report that those same individuals could not possibly have killer instinct, and ultimately, strong closing ability. If the tests picked up strong killer instinct as a dominant trait, then they were programmed to report that this person didn't have the ability to nurture, be nice, be warm and kind to people. The psychological tests had another shortcoming with regard to sales. They measured sales aptitude, or knowledge, which doesn't have any correlation to predicting outcomes. An individual can know a tremendous amount of information about many things. You see them in sports all of the time. Analysts, experts and gurus. Many of them never played professionally! It's the same in sales. Sales knowledge won't turn you into a closer. Sales knowledge won't give you those magical people skills. Sales knowledge won't make you wealthy. Only your ability to execute will assure those results.

"Employing the principals of Mindless Selling enables you to be the captain of your ship."

Dave Kurlan

I learned something else very surprising - Given a choice between an emotionally unbalanced, somewhat "messed up" individual, who would produce sales with consistency, or a well balanced, emotionally stable salesperson who couldn't sell his way out of a paper bag, I preferred the basket case! So I developed my own sales - based evaluation, that provided me with information that was crucial to the growth and development of salespeople, and just as importantly, an evaluation which was user-friendly. That one difference allowed me to focus my training efforts on fixing problems instead of only sharing techniques. I was able to help salespeople develop a comfort level with the process, rather than confusing them with more new ways to close. I showed them why they got the results they got, as well as how they got them, rather then having to tell them that one way was better than another. I achieved results when other trainers were getting standing ovations. I provided substance while other trainers provided fluff. I enlightened and empowered people when others were busy dazzling them with show biz productions. I was determined to be different.

It is in that spirit of difference and refreshment that I present my thoughts on selling in this book. I did not intend for this to be another one of the already too many "how to close every sale" books. It is not a book offering "888 new ways to handle objections." It is not a manual on "how to book appointments with anyone over the telephone." Nor is it a book on "how to make winning presentations", "how to develop relationships with prospects and customers", or "how to write a winning proposal." After all, what good is one more technique, when the techniques that are already in existence often don't work? What good is another technique on handling objections if you aren't comfortable being in a situation where you have to handle an objection in the first place? What good is one more closing technique if you feel pressure when the prospect

3

"An intellectual is a man who takes more words than necessary to tell more than he knows."

Dwight D. Eisenhower

gives you stalls at closing time? What good is another selling system if you can't execute the one you're using now?

It is for these reasons that I have written this book on how to become a complete salesperson. Nearly all of the books written invite you to learn "new", "proven", "powerful", "innovative", "systematic" approaches to "handling" the same problems that have been around since people became involved in selling. I don't believe that we need to reinvent the science of selling. I believe we need to help people with the implementation side of selling. You and everyone you meet are capable of learning the science of selling, the part that dictates, "do this, this, this, and then that." Many people, and you may be one of them, have learned the science of selling and know what they're supposed to do and when they're supposed to do it. The problem is that they are quite probably unable to execute any more effectively than you or I could play NBA basketball after a lecture on how to "slam dunk." Your knowledge of selling as a process is not enough to help you execute effectively on a daily basis.

With the information in this book, you will discover the tools you'll need to make important changes within and to facilitate the process of becoming a more effective salesperson. I give you this rather than suggesting that you merely say the things that effective salespeople say. You will learn what it takes to win in sales, rather than just how to say what the winners say. You can shoot a basketball like Larry Bird, but that won't help you compete at the NBA level. It won't even get the ball to fall in the hoop consistently. First, you must become what Larry Bird was. Sports writers and his teammates in Boston called Larry Bird a competitor who couldn't stand to lose. He was a team player with exceptional peripheral vision, incredible basketball instinct, and respect for the game and its other players while commanding their respect in return. He was a

"What good is one more technique on handling objections if you aren't comfortable being in a situation where you have to handle an objection in the first place?"

Dave Kurlan

leader and a student. He practiced more than most other accomplished athletes due to his drive and ambition. It wasn't unusual for Larry to practice his shooting for three hours a day - on game days! He made a lot of money and earned every penny of it, especially in championship games when he consistently rose to the occasion under tremendous pressure. He performed best when money was on the line. He was one of the finest passers in the game even though he wasn't a guard. Despite not being seven feet tall, he rebounded as well as the giants in the game. Although Larry was not blessed with great speed he covered the floor as well as anyone ever did. He was the all time complete basketball player. But how did he become the best? Did someone merely show him how to shoot, pass, jump, guard and leave the rest to chance? Can someone merely give you a system with several techniques and expect you to become a world class professional salesperson?

If you take this book to heart, you will develop the inner strength, wisdom, character, competitiveness, and spirit to execute with the best. When you become the complete salesperson, you won't need sales crutches, the hundreds of techniques used by the amateur salespeople of the world. You'll be able to throw the techniques out the window and sell effortlessly and effectively.

When you employ mindless selling you will find yourself exclusively in the moment. You will no longer be thinking several moves ahead, planning strategies, preparing questions, and fretting objections. When you employ mindless selling, you won't be struggling to listen over the endless dialogue of mind clutter that permeates your brain cells. You won't be worrying about what was or wasn't said fifteen minutes ago. When you employ mindless selling, you will be in total control, every step of the way. You'll have that control because you'll be prepared to have that control.

The consummate professional is ready for everything and doesn't need to over-think a selling situation.

In the upcoming chapters you will not only learn and develop the attitudes, characteristics and behaviors needed to be a winning salesperson, but you'll learn how to control your thoughts, improve your listening skills, and have total control whenever you want it. I hope you enjoy becoming the best as much as you enjoy the rewards that being the best will bring.

"Nothing in the world can take the place of persistence. Talent will not; nothing is more common than unsuccessful men with talent."

Calvin Coolidge

BOREDOM SETS IN

2

"Some people may not be right for sales. I'd like to save them from failing in sales when there may be so very much at stake."

Dave Kurlan

I don't like to categorize people, but during the last twenty-two years I have noticed common traits that affect people's ability to adapt well to sales. Most people become salespeople purely by accident. Recently, I was helping a client hire two salespeople. Prior to my involvement in the process, they solicited resumes from various applicants. Resumes have their place toward the end of the hiring process, and I have several reasons for staying away from them at the beginning, a few of which I'll mention here for managers who involve themselves in the selection process.

In my opinion, the first error that many companies make in the hiring process occurs when they place an ad which clearly states, "send resume to..." That may sound harmless enough, but if you're looking for a salesperson who will get on the phone and prospect, you won't typically find that person through a resume search. Instead, you'll get a pile of paper from thankful wimps, equipped with beautiful resumes, purchased from their neighborhood resume store. I don't have anything against the resume preparers or the candidates that send the resumes when asked. I think it's important that if you place an ad seeking a salesperson who, among other things, will be expected to get on the phone and prospect for appointments, that the only way to determine whether he will get on that phone, as well as how effective he'll be, is to have this candidate call you! You'll get a chance to see whether the individual has the ability to identify you, the decision maker, whether he can get through to you, and if so, how the individual sounds on the phone and how effectively he handles pressure. (Of course you will put pressure on this individual.) My second problem with early requests for resumes is that effective salespeople often fail to have resumes which, when compared to the rest of the pack, are attractive. While this isn't true 100% of the time, some of the finest salespeople I've encountered don't pay much attention to paperwork, of which the resume is a close relative. Some salespeople are so hungry, so ambitious, and so driven that they see paperwork as a distraction to the actual game of selling. Could this salesperson be a liability to your company? Only if you fail to hire him. You may have to equip this seller with a sales assistant because you certainly won't change his ways, but you'll probably be more tempted to hire someone who completes their paperwork to your satisfaction. Just remember that the cost of a sales assistant, spread among all of your salespeople, will pale in comparison to the additional business a motivated seller like this will generate.

Salespeople like this are often overlooked and denied interviews from people in personnel who are professionally trained to examine resumes! Susan, who was the Personnel director for one of my clients put resumes into three piles. "Yes's" were the resumes which were professionally typeset, and included specific industry experience.

"Noes" were made up of resumes that were obviously typed at home and those that belonged to salespeople who lacked industry specific experience. The "maybes" all had nice resumes, industry experience, but seemed to lack a track record. Clearly, some of the resumes in the "yes" pile were good candidates, but most weren't! Obviously, some of the resumes in the "no" pile were poor candidates for any job, but many belonged to exceptional salespeople! Such a pity.

While sifting through another client's pile of resumes, one factor was very obvious to me. The ad sought out sales engineers and since the applicants were primarily engineers my client was predictably impressed with the number of responses as well as the technical expertise of the applicants. Like so many others who hire salespeople, he failed to notice that applicants state their objective at the top of the resume and in this case, those objectives didn't exactly

"All you need in this life is ignorance and confidence, and then success is sure."

Mark Twain

match the position. The objective often reads something like this: "I seek an entry level engineering position with a growing company where there is opportunity for advancement and the ability to use those skills which I have developed in my previous experience."

What so many managers fail to recognize is that there isn't anything missing from the objective. These individuals are not seeking out a career in sales; they are engineers who wish to do engineering. Because of corporate downsizing in the high tech industries during the first half of the nineties, laid off technical people are having difficulty finding work, so they often apply for the position of sales engineer, write a cover letter that begins with "I am applying for the position of sales engineer as advertised in the Boston Globe on Sunday", and gladly accept the position if it is offered to them. Eight months later, no one in the company can figure out why Eugene, the technical whiz, is struggling so badly!

Eugene is an example of an individual who arrives in sales by accident and is completely unprepared for the cruelties he will encounter in his new career. Others like Eugene move into sales as a way of keeping a job with their company. One day, they awaken from bed as they always do, shower, brush, shave, read the paper, have breakfast, get in the car, go to work like they have for years, only to learn that the company is changing its focus or direction. As a result of this change in philosophy, several things have happened. One is that the opportunity for an engineer to advance in this company has been all but eliminated. The second is a series of employee layoffs, the third is a freeze on wages, and the fourth, an "opportunity" for people like Eugene to slide into sales, if they wish to remain with the company. There he'll have an opportunity to earn the same or more than he was pulling in as an engineer. Eugene picks number four and the adventure begins!

A large group of people find that they aren't qualified to do any kind of skilled work, which pays well, and they aren't excited about taking an unskilled job that pays poorly, so they go into sales, totally unprepared for a career in selling. The following comments represent my experiences after working with salespeople who moved from a non-selling career into sales, and how trainable I found them to be. While this isn't the gospel, it may help those who are contemplating a change, as well as those managers who must interview sales candidates with no prior sales experience.

By far, the profession from which a successful change to sales is least likely is purchasing agent or buyer. For reasons explained in the chapter entitled Peddlers, purchasing agents use a process that contradicts every necessary mind-set required for success in sales. I have not yet interviewed a sales candidate from the purchasing world who had the ability to succeed in sales, nor have I trained a converted purchasing agent who would do anything other than fight with the process.

I probably need to define "succeed" as it applies to selling. My definition of success in sales is when an individual develops, maintains, and grows a book of business to the point where he is in the top 10% in his industry. There are many people who make a lot of money in sales, but it's often due to being in the right place at the right time.

For instance, Charlie was a self made success in sales, started from scratch in the printing business, built a territory from zero, grew the business within that territory, and maintained it as well, for over thirty years! Now Charlie's retiring and Willy, an ex-printer with two years of experience in the insurance business, is taking over Charlie's territory.

If Willy was any good at selling, he'd still be in the insurance business, so it's pretty safe to assume that Willy had failed. Second, he's not only taking over Charlie's territory, he's also taking over Charlie's commission check! And not only that, but because of the number of customers in the territory, Willy won't even have to go out and prospect for new business.

Most people will look at Willy and say, "boy, did he become successful." In reality, he became lucky! Now if he had a smart manager, that manager would have told Willy to go out and find some business, and for every new account that Willy brought in, his manager would give him one of Charlie's old accounts as a reward. Too bad most managers aren't smarter.

If you happen to be a career purchasing agent and you feel tempted to earn the money that those "sleazy" salespeople earn, make another wish! Your negative perception of salespeople alone should provide the million dollar clue that a career in sales is not in the offering for you.

The second career from which it is unlikely to make a successful entry into sales, is that of social worker. Social workers have technical training in the arts of listening, asking questions, and nurturing. These three skills are highly desirable for selling. The nurturing keeps a prospect from feeling threatened and hides the impact of tough questions. The questions themselves help prospects discover what their real problems are, and a skilled salesperson can uncover a wealth of information with regard to how to sell this prospect, what to sell this prospect, and why this prospect will buy. But before a question can be formulated, the seller must have keen listening skills. He must hear what is truly being said, as opposed to what the prospect wants him to hear, or what the salesperson himself wishes to hear.

Despite having mastered these three skills, social workers tend to be very survival oriented rather than money motivated. People who wish to earn a lot of money don't often make social work a career choice. Folks who choose social work usually have a desire to help, to give, to be of service to people more needy than they are. While this is very generous and important in our society, the lack of desire to make a lot of money and the lack of killer instinct are two limitations that are often insurmountable. Most of the social workers turned salespeople who I've met have not been competitive people driven by a motivation to win. I don't mean to imply that you must be an athlete or even a fan of professional sports in order to succeed

11

in sales. However, there is a connection between success in sales and killer instinct, and the ex-social worker typically doesn't possess the latter.

A client, who later came to work for my sales training firm, was a counselor. Arnie had been a top-notch insurance salesperson on the West Coast before heading east with his family to take up real estate. By the time he met me, his best earning years were a distant memory and his struggles had just begun. I don't like people who make excuses for their failures and in the late eighties and early nineties most Realtors had more excuses than listings. Arnie wasn't one of those complainers, and as a matter of fact, he was a very positive, very warm person. One thing Arnie had that his counterparts lacked was religion. I think that having a religion to embrace is a wonderful thing. It's important for all of us to have something or someone to believe in. In Arnie's case, his desire to become a Deacon in the Catholic Church and his subsequent appointment to the position coincided with his downfall in sales.

His once strong killer instinct left him behind and he replaced it with his problem solving mentality. Salespeople who are good problem solvers usually do quite well, as the skill is a tremendous asset, but when salespeople begin solving problems that aren't their concern they usually pay the price. Arnie's cost was his inability to earn commissions and its terrible impact on his personal finances. His products and services were very appropriate for his prospects, and they would never find anyone with stronger integrity than his. Rather than addressing the problems he could solve through his real estate business, he was trying to improve everyone's life...without their permission! All they had to do was give a little indication that there may be slight problem with some part of their life and Arnie would immediately become "Super Deacon". Time for Arnie to "help." It was the end of the two-way dialogue. There was no opportunity for the prospect to speak. The end of the sales call came quickly. There was no chance for a commission. In the terrorizing words of the error message displayed by my word processor, "! Unrecoverable Application Error!"

Arnie could no longer separate life from sales, an absolute deathblow to a salesperson. He couldn't close anyone whom he suspected had a problem, or more appropriately, told him a sob story. Talk about taking stalls and put offs! Despite Arnie's vast storehouse of information, his knowledge of closing, his prior successes, and his ability to recognize a stall from a promise, he had become a sucker for the prospect's all time ten best tricks.

The Ten Best Tricks That Prospect Use:

1. Stall for time.
2. Form a committee.
3. Make up an objection.
4. Pretend to be unable to afford it.
5. Claim to have been offered a better deal from someone else.
6. Pretend he has to talk it over with someone first.
7. Claim to be unable to make decisions the first time he sees something.
8. Suggest that the salesperson will have to offer a better price.
9. Claim to be unsure of what they actually want to do at this point in time.
10. Imply that they simply don't need it, don't want it, or don't like it.

Technicians of various expertises fall into my third category of those most likely to be unsuccessful in sales. These experts know so much about their field that they usually can't keep their mouth shut long enough to learn that everything they know isn't important to their prospect. Jason is a good example of this particular sales misfit. He was so concerned with covering each and every detail of the product that he was unable to observe the simplest of clues from his prospect. If he were paying close enough attention to notice that they might be in disharmony over a suggestion he made, he would defend his suggestion to the death rather than defend his prospect's right to their opinion. Technical accuracy took precedent over everything, including his ability to keep the prospect comfortable. Since his analytical skills far outweighed his people skills, he spent more time trying to "figure out" what was happening to him and attempting to "read" the situation than he did asking questions to determine how to solve the prospect's problems, or how to sell the prospect.

Most technical people will argue that they do know how to sell, and it's unfair of me to categorize them this way. Well, they're right. They may know how to sell, but their inability to follow the sales process and execute is often a problem. Jason "learned" how to sell, and well enough to pass his new found knowledge on to his wife, who was also fairly new to sales. Donna not only learned from Jason, but excelled! She quickly became a top salesperson in her region despite being new, proof enough that Jason not only learned, but also sufficiently internalized it to teach it effectively. Despite his teaching success, Jason's many internal limitations still prevented him from being able to execute effectively, not unlike the thousands of other technical experts contemplating a career in sales.

The teacher is a professional who often turns to sales. They're usually good with people, they learn to make excellent presentations, and often have a wonderful work ethic. Teachers run into problems with the rules of selling. Most of the rules contradict everything they taught, for instance: Answering a question with a question. A social worker understands the importance of answering a question with a question because instead of dealing with a smoke screen or a symptom, they can deal with a real problem. Most teachers see something like that as a highly unnecessary gimmick. While the professional salesperson knows to remain quiet, listen, often play dumb, and always ask good questions, the teacher needs to educate. That makes the teacher highly vulnerable to prospects who want to pick a salesperson's brain, kick tires, comparison shop, or as their sales managers see it, provide unpaid consulting.

The fifth category of people who I contend don't make great salespeople are people who hate salespeople. Doug was an insurance salesperson who visited me just prior to the Persian Gulf War. He had spent the last seven years selling insurance. He had more knowledge of the business than anyone I had ever met; yet his income had peaked at $27,000! It is very unusual for someone with his knowledge and tenure to remain at the same income level for three years running. For the uninformed, a mediocre insurance salesperson has the ability to earn well over $50,000 after five years, and a moderately successful agent will go over $100,000. Also keep in mind that the insurance industry is its own worst enemy, for it applauds mediocrity, and accepts failure. I often have insurance people come to me for help and relate that the boss says that they're doing really well - despite their paltry $18,000 earnings. Or, they've been told that they're second in production for the entire office. What I want to know is, second to what?

I had to find out why Doug was performing so poorly before I could help him. The reason for his poor showing was his primary motivation for entering sales. He had developed a hatred for salespeople following several bad experiences that he and his wife shared. Once, they were "pressured" into purchasing a time share property. Despite the fact that I don't believe that anyone can be pressured into buying anything, it was his perception that they were pressured. People must learn to become more effective getting that difficult two letter word, "no", out of their mouth!

On another occasion they were sold a car which qualified for the lemon law. I've purchased eleven new cars in my lifetime and I'd bet a handful of hundreds that eight of them had enough problems to qualify for that stupid law if I really wanted to take the time and energy to raise a fuss. Aren't cars supposed to have things go wrong with them? If cars ran the way they were supposed to, that would take all the fun out of owning one, wouldn't it?

The third event was truly tragic. Doug's infant daughter was very sick, having to be taken to the hospital on numerous occasions. On the most recent trip it became apparent that she wasn't going to pull through like she had before. Doug and his wife were devastated! On the day of their infant daughter's funeral, an unsuspecting life insurance salesperson called to sell them a policy to insure her life. Doug determined right then and there that the insurance world would be a little nicer if he were part of it.

Unfortunately for Doug, his obsession with honesty, as well as his commitment to be different turned him into an educator. People found him boring. He was sympathetic to their excuses, but unresponsive to their needs. He was always selling at the lowest price, but with inadequate solutions. He was extremely well liked, but equally unsuccessful. He refused to do anything that he perceived as "sales like." He wouldn't ask questions because he thought them to be intrusive. He wouldn't talk about money because he thought it to be invasive. Doug would never be successful because he wasn't dedicated to helping people get what they truly needed to solve their problems. He was dedicated to providing an alternate sales approach to the ones which he disliked so intensely. Because of one shady salesperson in a time-share resort, a defective car, and a salesperson who chose the wrong family to prospect, Doug was doomed to endure an unsuccessful career in sales, doing the wrong things for the wrong reasons, and getting results that he could not comprehend. Doug is not alone.

There are many people who would make fine salespeople and there are many more that would not. My purpose is not to discourage anyone from entering sales, but to raise the awareness of those who may have stumbled into selling for the wrong reasons, or with an abundance of self limiting perceptions. I'd like to help those people who may not be right for sales. The frustration of giving it the old college try, when there may be much more at risk than there was back in college, leaves you empty and discouraged, feeling like a failure.

Ideally, I would like to give everyone involved in the profession of selling an understanding of what it takes to be the best, something that is most easily accomplished by giving examples of those horrors which prevent people from becoming the best.

Stories like those belonging to Arnie, Doug and Jason are just a few of the examples I'll share with you in the upcoming chapters. You may recognize yourself in some of these tales of woe. If you do, don't panic. If you are truly committed to a career in sales, any obstacles you may uncover in this book can be overcome. If you don't recognize yourself anywhere, congratulate yourself, and then make sure you're earning enough money for someone who is obstacle free.   If you're not, start the book over again and determine with which limitations you're in denial. Yeah, that's the ticket!

THE RAW BAR

3

"Your ability to speak conversationally rather than grammatically will aid you in your quest."

Dave Kurlan

There are certain raw abilities which, when possessed by salespeople, help them to be more effective than the rest of the crowd. I call them raw because they are very difficult to teach, learn, or develop. They are pure people skills, imperative for sales success. The winners possess all of them, while those who lack some or all of these abilities struggle to a greater degree.

Natural Eye Contact- I'm not speaking about the individual who can lock his pupils on someone else's pupils without blinking or turning away. That description, one often used to describe people who are trustworthy, is myth. Most who have this "stare right through" you ability are good cons! When I talk about natural, this means they can look right at their prospect when they are talking to their prospect, but still look away naturally to process information, or to "look up" the answers to questions, as well as to think. Natural eye contact allows for significant eye movement, something that is very normal and often comfortable for a prospect. One's ability to maintain natural eye contact will help an individual to appear trustworthy.

Non Threatening Appearance - You don't have to pack a pistol, look like an undesirable, or be a leather and chain clad member of a motorcycle gang to appear threatening to your prospect. An abundance of confidence, extremely powerful clothing, arrogance, extra weight, extra height, or a successful reputation may all contribute to a prospect that feels uncomfortable with you. Their discomfort translates into your dismay, disjune, and disjuly when you can't lower the barriers placed between you and your prospect. A low-key demeanor is very desirable. When in doubt about dress, try

"Forget everything you learned in school about grammar. If you're talking with a prospect, especially during presentations, you must keep it simple, informal, short, and to the point if you wish to avoid becoming a threat..."

Dave Kurlan

to wear what you believe your prospect might wear, but dress down one notch so as not to be in competition for best dressed. It's very important that you not play the "I'm better than you are" game. When in doubt, dress down, not up. Any barriers you create by dressing down will be much easier to break through than the barriers created by looking too much like a killer salesperson!

Good Tonality- This is the single most difficult piece to fix. It takes the vocal flexibility of a good impressionist to change the texture of the voice. Some people have tonality that is naturally warm and nurturing. Women tend to sound warmer and more nurturing than their male counterparts but of course there are exceptions in both genders. Those folks who have been cursed with an abrasive sounding voice will have a great deal of difficulty in coming across as nurturing. The ability to nurture is created by a somewhat slower pace, softer volume, lower pitch, and most significantly, inflection, a drop in pitch of the last syllable of the final word in a thought or phrase. This is accomplished by correctly pronouncing "Be-bop", the popular style of jazz in the late 50's. Nurturing is important because without prospects will have difficulty being asked tough questions, which by themselves tend to put pressure on a prospect. Mastering the art of nurturing helps you to ask questions that sound more like statements or gentle instructions to your prospect, rather than having the telltale question mark at the end be the last punctuation your prospect hears. Your ability to speak conversationally rather than grammatically will aid you in your quest. Forget everything you learned in school about grammar. If you're talking with a prospect, especially during presentations, you must keep it simple, informal, short, and to the point if you wish to maintain their interest while not becoming a threat. Your ability to combine a nurturing tonality with trustworthiness will help you to appear to be extremely sincere.

The best salespeople are able to fake sincerity, understanding that genuine sincerity may cause them to become emotionally involved. It's best to go the way of doctors, talk show hosts, and actors who always fake sincerity. Notice how the top talk show hosts never brag about what they have as one upsmanship is out of the question. Your prospect should always have more of everything than you should. If you find out that they have a boat and you want to talk about boats, make sure that you talk about how much you've always wanted a boat like theirs! It's equally important to love, or at least like everything your prospect does, says, and believes in. Your ability to fake sincerity will keep you out of trouble and at least prevent you from buying back what you just sold! This means always keeping your ego in check! Your ego is that part of you who always wants to correct a prospect when they're wrong, who wants to show how much you know, who wants to brag, who wants to be recognized for what you've done. Well, forget it!

There is a living, breathing example of the nurturing individual you should strive to imitate. He hosts one of the most listened to radio talk shows in the USA. Tune in to Bruce Williams on Talknet, an affiliate station you're sure to find on your AM dial any weekday evening between the hours of 7pm and 10pm EST. He is the master of nurture, fake sincerity, tough question after tough question, and he never upsets his callers. I haven't heard anyone consistently demonstrate this ability better than Bruce. As an added bonus, listen to how effectively and consistently he plays dumb. This allows him to uncover additional information, from which further questioning can be developed. It also keeps his caller's defenses down, as they continue to talk about their problems, instead of listening to him solve them. Many talk show hosts can't wait to solve their caller's problems, often failing to uncover the real problem along the way. Salespeople can learn an awful lot about selling from Bruce Williams, even though he's not teaching it!

A nice smile- As unorthodox as my beliefs are, I still believe in a smile that shows teeth. Your warm smile combined with the sincerity and trustworthiness developed with your good natural eye contact, your non-threatening appearance, and your nurturing tonality will radiate warmth. Warmth is that good feeling you have when you know your spouse loves you. Warmth is that good feeling you had as a small child when you knew your parents cared for you. Warmth is that feeling which comes over you when you are reunited with dear friends after not seeing them for a long time. Warmth makes your prospect believe you care about helping them. I believe that this is a very significant part of selling. When you combine all of these traits, you will have discovered the secret of salespeople who learned to sell strictly on the merits of their wonderful personality. These pieces of the puzzle will allow you to develop rapport very quickly with your prospects. Rapport, along with bonding, is important enough to represent at least 50% of a prospect's motivation to do business with you.

Bonding while complimentary to rapport, is different because while rapport helps you find common ground, it must be redeveloped each time you meet with your prospect or customer. Bonding, once established, sticks "like glue", the proof being your friends and family members, (the MCI group), with whom you have that magic connection even when you aren't there. After not seeing a friend or a close family member for months or years, the feeling you get when you are reunited is strong enough to have withstood all the time that you were out of touch. That's bonding. That's important in selling. That's something you should learn how to establish if you haven't already mastered a technique called mirroring. While there are many books that talk about bonding and rapport building techniques, many are somewhat watered down for the general masses. If you want to go straight to the horse's mouth, a hard to find book, called "Frogs Into Princes", by Richard Bandler and John Grinder, published by Real People Press, will demonstrate through case histories, exactly how to go about this process.

The real pros that stand out for their ability to develop bonding and/or rapport are truly unforgettable. I'll never forget Len, who lit up every room he ever entered whose hobby was traveling to far corners of the globe in order to ride the finest roller coasters in the world! I won't forget Marc, who made futile weekly attempts at getting me to go sailing with him every week. I won't forget Joe, who not only took me bass fishing, but also showed me how to catch big large mouth bass. Then there was John, who delivered a summer's worth of beef and chicken for the grill, Guy who regularly gave me season tickets to Red Sox games, Jeremiah, who sent me his "state of the family" letter each New Year, and so many more. These people aren't mentioned here because they gave me things to remember. They are remembered because they learned how to get close enough to me so that I would accept the things they wanted to give me. There are many more that tried to give but weren't allowed. There are even more who never tried. If you haven't mastered your bonding and rapport skills, you've shut the door to fifty percent of the selling process.

PHONE HOME

4

"Those who suffer from low self esteem often have poor attitudes, and even more frequently, they make excuses for their performance or lack thereof."

Dave Kurlan

I remember the scene in the movie ET where ET and his young companion ride off on a bicycle, an unforgettable image of the two shadowing the moon. Up there in space, with gravity safely out of their way, they could go anywhere. The sky was no longer the limit, their destiny only a bi-product of their imagination. Life in sales is similar, because there isn't anything to hold us back other than the limits of our imagination, and our need to discount our dreams.

There are several important elements that, when present in a positive way, contribute to a successful sales career. When these elements are present in a negative way or not there at all, they suggest that a career would be better in another field.

We'll look at the elements in the order of their effect on you, but not in their order of importance. Your destination, or how clearly you can see your dreams and your goals, is vitally important. With clear focus as to what you want from life, where you might want to live, the kind of house you dream of owning, the car you wish to drive, the grown up toys you'd like to play with, the traveling you wish to do, the people you want to spend your time with, the things you want to spend your time doing, the amount of free time you'd like to have, the amount of money you'll need in order to retire, the age at which you'd like to retire, the hobbies you'd like to take up, the interests you'd like to develop, the things you'd like to provide for your family, and even what you want to be when you grow up (again), you'll have every reason to sell enthusiastically and passionately.

"An earnest desire to succeed is almost always prognostic of success."

King of Poland

You must set your compass. While few people actually have dreams and goals that have been put to paper complete with realization dates, the work doesn't stop there. Even fewer people take the time to work out a plan of achievement, one which when followed, will actually lead them right to their goals and dreams.

After you know what you truly want from life you must set short term goals for the next twelve months, which when reached, will bring you closer to your dreams. These goals represent those things you can accomplish in the next year, which start the process of reaching your dreams, or things you wish to buy, or places you wish to go. The cost of these goals must be determined and broken down monthly. Your total monthly expenses should be added to the monthly cost of your goals so that a total cost of monthly expenses can be determined. This number, let's say $10,000, should be divided by the actual number of income producing days you have each month, say 15. $10,000 divided by 15 days is equal to $666 per day, the amount of money you must earn each day. If you have a base salary, income from residual sales, or income from a spouse, say $5000, or $333 per day, that amount can be subtracted from the $666, leaving just $333 per day that must be earned in commissions.

Next, we must determine exactly what activity will be required of you in order to earn $333 in a day. This can be accomplished by taking your average commission (average sale times average percentage of commission), let's say $500 and dividing it into the daily income requirement, $333. In this example .67 is the answer, meaning you must make .67 sales per day. Using your own historical data, you must determine the following: How many quotes or proposals for one sale? How many prospects must you meet with to generate one proposal? How many appointments must you book to meet with one prospect? (This must account for no shows cancellations and rescheduled appointments) How many prospects

"The road to success is always under construction."

Lily Tomlin

must you speak with by phone (or walk in cold) to book one appointment? How many times must you dial the phone in order to speak with one prospect? All of these answers should be multiplied by the previous answer in this example to determine actual activity. Now we have a plan and the compass is set.

Having progressed this far sets the stage for the single most important element in selling, your strong Desire for success. Until you have clear destination and compass, your desire won't be as strong. Without strong desire, you won't have the motivation to perform certain disliked selling activities which may lack glamour, such as cold calls, paperwork, dealing with difficult prospects, selling in a competitive market, and even doing things to shorten your selling cycle. By lacking desire, you'll have no reason to make changes to better yourself, or implement the knowledge gained from training, which could do wonders for your career.

With a clear destination and compass, as well as your strong desire, you now have something to commit to. Commitment is vitally important because without it, you won't do whatever it takes, "no matter what." It's the "no matter what" part that truly separates the committed from the non-committed. You must commit to your plan and everything that is required of you, including consistent daily execution, as well as the changes that you have agreed to make while reading this book, when going through training, or while planning how to achieve your dreams. It means doing everything you promised yourself you'd do, even if you're uncomfortable, even if you're afraid, even if you don't agree with the strategy, even if you perceive it to be too difficult.

Your consistent daily performance of the plan is considered to be an Exercise Program of sorts, and without it you can't effectively track your progress. Not only is tracking vital to your success, it will also serve to predict exactly what you can expect for sales n days into the future, with n being the number of days in your sell cycle.

25

David Kurlan

"For Glory gives herself only to those who have always dreamed of her."

Charles DeGaulle

We compute n by determining the average number of days that pass from the date of first contact with your prospect to the date of closing. As an example, let's say that n is sixty, and in its simplest form our plan calls for us to have contacted twenty new prospects this week, booked six first meetings, and made four final presentations or closes. We already know from history that when we do this, based on our current level of skill, we will bring in y sales, worth an average of $x each, which is exactly what our plan calls for us to do. If we perform our exercise program this week as specified, then we know that sixty days from now, we'll have $2x in sales. Conversely, if we fail to perform the exercise program as specified, falling short in any of the categories, then sixty days from now we'll also fall short of the $2x called for in our plan.   Consistent performance of your exercise program is vital!

Your outlook, which encompasses self-image and accountability, is vitally important as well. Those who suffer from low self-esteem often have poor attitudes, and even more frequently, they make excuses for their performance or lack thereof. These people are often viewed as complainers, trouble makers, or know it alls, but often their numbers aren't up to snuff. I have found that once a salesperson has clear destination and compass, the desire to reach their goals, a commitment to their plan, and they have begun execution of their exercise program, outlook improves significantly. As soon as we begin to feel better about ourselves, we become more confident and our bravery improves.

Bravery is essential, for without it we are unable to execute the most difficult of techniques, those that present some form of risk for the salesperson. The better you feel, the stronger you'll be. The stronger you are, the more effective you will be with your style. There is an expression in the sport of bullfighting used to describe the matador, standing firm in the center of the arena, awaiting the

26

"With a strong enough desire for success and a commitment to do whatever it takes, most people are capable of overcoming any obstacle in order to succeed."

Dave Kurlan

oncoming charge of the bull. The expression is ver llagen (bear jagen) which translates literally into "to see it coming", or in the world of the matador, "to see the bull coming", which to me, seems to describe the art of selling better than any other expression I have ever heard. To see the bull coming, and to dig in, plant your feet, and hang with the bull the prospect throws your way. Yup, that's professional selling!

Style is the combination of your technique and your personality, along with your ability to establish bonding with people. It is the least important element of success because it is the easiest to learn or acquire. Unfortunately, it is the least understood of all of the elements, because many people believe that style is the only thing you need in order to be effective. Technique is influenced by your Record Collection, your collection of both supportive and self-limiting messages that relate to the selling process, so powerful that they actually predetermine your actions and your sales outcomes. This is what I affectionately refer to as the music of selling.

Over the years I have seen many salespeople who knew what they were supposed to do, when they were supposed to do it, and to whom they were supposed to do it. They could tell both of us how to handle the most delicate of situations. They understood the science of selling. They had a system. Psychological evaluations tell them that they have sales know-how. These are the people who can sell, but they aren't always the ones who do sell. One difference between can and will is a self limiting record collection. To give you an idea as to how all of these elements play together, I'll relate a story about a salesperson with who I once worked.

Bill was thin, balding, wore clothes that were too large, and had a poor complexion. To make matters worse he spoke as if he had marbles in his mouth and tried much too hard to get people to like

"The dictionary is the only place where success comes before work."

Arthur Brisbane

him. He walked like a wimp, talked like a wimp, acted like a wimp, looked like a wimp, and frankly, he was a genuine wimp!

Bill's prior sales position was that of rug salesman. He worked for his father's mill where they manufactured area rugs. Bill called on department stores and basically asked them what color and which size they wanted to reorder. His actual knowledge of selling was non existent and he had no other particular strengths from which to draw.

Bill had no particular goals at this point in his life, he wasn't particularly money motivated, he was content with his apartment and happy with his Honda Civic. He rarely dated, wasn't effective when socializing and he led an extremely boring life. He had no destination or compass.

Bill's picture would have been perfect for the title page on the chapter for low self esteem in Psychology 101. Due largely to his domineering father, who constantly reminded him that he'd never amount to anything, Bill hadn't amounted to anything. Thanks to his father's recent death, Bill no longer had a job, was mourning the father he had a love/hate/intimidate relationship with, and felt like a complete failure for not amounting to anything. Add to that his failures with women, like his first fiancée dumping him for postponing the wedding - due to his father's impending death. "Your father had to pick now to die? And of all the times for you to become emotionally unstable - Well!" was what she probably said to him. Or his second fiancée, who stole his money and his jewelry before leaving town without a trace. In terms of outlook, Bill had very little.

Since Bill lacked destination, there was a complete lack of commitment because he didn't have any real goals or dreams to which he could commit. There wasn't an exercise program to follow since there wasn't a plan. Bill lacked technique, personality, and a

28

selling system, so he was essentially without a style. He was a big wimp and didn't have any bravery. He was even more pitiful when it came to record collection, possessing every self limiting record known to man, and lacking every supportive record which could have helped him out. The only thing Bill had was desire, and that wasn't immediately evident.

After some soul searching, (It was me searching his soul), I found that there was more than a little resentment for his father. I also learned that he would have loved to prove his father wrong about not amounting to anything. When I asked what would have happened if he could have proved that he was worthy of his father's respect, he told me that he would have been the happiest person on earth. When I asked him how important it would have been to him, he told me that nothing would have been more important. With that we found the magic, the one thing that was more powerful than any skill, more potent than any technique, more motivating than any car or boat. We found his desire!

A salesperson can be lacking in destination, compass, outlook, exercise program, style, record collection, and bravery. If there is a strong enough desire to be successful, along with a commitment to do whatever it takes, then most people are capable of overcoming any obstacle to succeed. Bill was no exception. Lacking in every conceivable way, Bill was about to prove that strong desire and commitment were indeed enough.

I still had one obstacle to take care of regarding Bill. Where in God's name could I have him sell? I certainly couldn't recommend him to a client and he surely wasn't capable of hitting the streets and landing a sales position on his own. So what then? I did what any savvy businessperson would do. I hired him, but without any expectation that he would develop business. In the sales training business, no one will spend one red cent on a training program if they don't perceive that the trainer or his sales rep was significantly stronger than the best salesperson on his team. Bill certainly wouldn't meet that expectation, so I assigned him to a territory where he couldn't hurt me and we began the metamorphosis.

"The dictionary is the only place where success comes before work."

Arthur Brisbane

After setting goals, writing a plan, committing to the plan and beginning his exercise program, Bill was on his way. It wasn't a very good start though. At first, Bill had problems worse than getting past secretaries. They were hanging up on him. Remember that he didn't speak very well. It wasn't long though before he was able to talk with secretaries, but couldn't get through to decision-makers. That was followed by a time where he got through to presidents but was promptly hung up on. By the beginning of the second month, Bill was able to have a conversation with the president of the company, but it would always end with a disinterested prospect. Six weeks had passed and he still didn't have an appointment, but he wasn't discouraged. In fact, he was growing stronger every day! He was beginning to see the progress he was making, the change in his voice, and the change in his confidence. More importantly he learned not to take any of this personally.

With continued persistence he finally reached the point where he could have intelligent conversations with prospects and book an appointment to see them, only to have them cancel, reschedule, no show, or kick him out when he got there. When he did finally make stronger appointments, his prospects were too tough for him and the calls went no where. By the fifth month, Bill was making effective sales calls, only to end up with a prospect that wouldn't do business with him. I sensed that this process was similar to taking a Chimpanzee and attempting to turn him into a salesperson. At this point I was sure Bill would sell. He had learned more about the art of selling than most salespeople ever would, and was only failing because he was trying to sell sales training, a tough enough sale for a seasoned trainer!

I was eating dinner in a hotel restaurant one evening when Bill suddenly appeared at my table. He must have made eighty or ninety phone calls to track me down, and then he had to drive two hours to get there. I looked at him and when I asked him what he was doing there he had the strangest grin on his face. I tell you, I've never seen anything like it in my life. It wasn't ear to ear, it was a 360o full circle beam! Absolutely the happiest man on planet earth was standing in front of me, and I still didn't know why. I thought he was about to tell me that he met a girl, fell in love, was getting married, won the lottery, gained five pounds, or, pray tell, did he sell someone?

He slapped a contract down on the table, and then, having finally sold a training program, he quit. He no longer had to prove anything to anyone. If he could sell sales training he could sell anything. Since he could sell, he didn't even have to be in sales. He could do anything. His father's ghost would haunt him no more!

Bill packed up his things and moved to Florida. His brother lived there year round and his mother resided there during the winter months. When he arrived he took a job in music therapy, an art for which he was trained. A music therapist travels to nursing homes and long term care facilities and provides several hours of participative, soothing music making for the residents. Bill was good at this, and if you remember my comments in chapter two about the career from which you shouldn't jump to sales, social work was one of the biggies.

After several months of music therapy, Bill asked his boss why they didn't have more accounts. She told him that no one had been calling for their services lately. He asked her why no one from the firm had been making sales calls. She told him that no one knew how to make sales calls. He said, "well I know something about that. Is it OK if I try it?"

"Sure", she said. Six months later, Bill had tripled their business. He added twenty-seven new accounts, and was expanding throughout Florida. He acquired an equity position in the company and became a partner. Three years later Bill was ready to begin franchising the music therapy business on a national scale. So his father was right. He never amounted to anything. He amounted to something!

One of the absolutely fascinating aspects about the words in our language is that they can mean whatever you chose to have them mean. Bill had been hearing this negative record playing around in his head for years, but when I played it, I found that it had been a positive record the entire time. You won't amount to anything; you'll amount to something! Which records have you been incorrectly interpreting all of these years?

PEDDLER
5

"It doesn't matter what anyone thinks of you, says about you, or feels toward you. The only two things that matter are that you have fun and get your prospect to do business with you."

Dave Kurlan

I find it truly amazing that the most important trait in selling is your ability to be a peddler. Of course there are two kinds of peddlers. One sells products door to door, and the other rides a bicycle. Funny, but some of the finest salespeople who ever lived considered themselves to be peddlers. These days, people look down upon peddlers as a form of low life scum sucking lizard or something nearly as awful as that. I was a peddler back in 1973, and my father was so embarrassed, he'd lay awake each night waiting for me to return home, and as I walked the stairs to my room he'd ask his daily question. "Did you sell any tonight?"

I figured that if I said yes, he'd become fearful that I might spend the next twenty years in sales. Of course I did, but that's another story. Actually, it is the story! I learned to say no, and then he'd bark that it was "probably for the best", and maybe now I could "go back to college and finish!" Then he'd go to sleep.

I was supposed to become an optometrist like him, join his practice, and examine eyes happily ever after. I can't blame him for this idea because it was all mine. Even though I dreamed of doing other things, like playing baseball for a living, I always thought that following in his footsteps was the proper thing to do. But I learned that you can't make other people happy, you have to please yourself first.

I learned it the hard way, and it took a long time to learn this most valuable lesson, but it was the single most important lesson. It doesn't matter what anyone thinks of you, says about you, feels toward you, or even, what they suggest to you. There are only two

"If you are shown a product and you can buy it right then and there, then with proper technique and bravery, you have the potential to be in closing encounters of the superstar kind."

Dave Kurlan

things that matter when it comes to selling. First, that you have fun, and second, that you get your prospect to do business with you.

You can't rise to the top of your class without burning some bridges; getting some people upset with you, and having some people dislike you. I'm not suggesting that you step on people or act in an unethical manner. I'm suggesting that you be your own person, create your own style, and attempt to be somewhat outrageous. In his book, *Confessions of an SOB,* Al Neuhearth sheds new light on outrageous behavior, and it's a very entertaining biography, one that every business person should be required to read.

I'd like to re-teach you the proper way to use a bicycle. Selling is a self-fulfilling prophecy. You will consistently get your prospects to behave in a manner that is consistent with how you would behave in a similar situation, or how you'd expect your prospect to behave. These expectations make up your Record Collection, or those permanently recorded messages that program your performance.

Peddling a bicycle may be the most important element in your Record Collection. First we change the spelling from bicycle to Buy Cycle. Use the same pronunciation as before, but place a tremendous degree of importance on your Buy Cycle. Your Buy Cycle or how you would normally go about the business of making a major purchase will predetermine the kind of sell cycle you will have when you sell to your prospects.

The ten crucial elements in your BuyCycle are:

1. Money Tolerance - At what dollar amount does something become a major purchase for you? _____. The lower this number is, the more vulnerable you will be to the objection "that's a lot of money." Your problem? You understand. The higher this number becomes, the more effective you will be at dealing with prospects who say this, because you will be less likely to understand their perception.

"Sometimes one pays more for the things one gets for nothing."
Albert Einstein

amount of time it could take you to get your prospect to do business with you. Your sell cycle will be longer than other salespeople in your industry will. Your prospect procrastinates, puts off making a decision, puts it on the back burner or says it isn't a priority. Your problem? You understand. The less time you invest in making a purchase, the harder it is for you to understand you'll make a better argument and your sell cycle will be shorter.

3. Potential for Getting Your Brain Picked for Free - Do you have a need to perform research before you buy? _____. If you research, visit salespeople to become educated, or you read Consumer Reports prior to buying, then you are extremely vulnerable to the prospect that wants to be educated. This prospect will usually pick your brain, determine what he needs, and then buy it from someone else for less money. You're liable to give too many inappropriate presentations. Your problem? You understand. If you don't have this need to perform research, you will have less tolerance for the prospect who wants to do it to you, and won't let him do it without some commitment that you'll do business together.

4. Competitive Vulnerability - How many stores will you shop, or how many salespeople will you invite in? ____. The more you need to comparison shop, the more you'll find yourself in that situation with your prospects. Your problem? You understand. If you can just go to one store and buy it, you'll have an easier time keeping the competition out of your way.

5. Profit Vulnerability - How do you decide from which store to purchase? _____. If you buy from the store where you can get the lowest price, you're in deep trouble here. You will be very vulnerable to the prospect that only buys the lowest price, where you will either cut profits to make the sale, or determine that you can't make the sales unless your price is lowered. Your problem? You understand. On the other hand, if you choose from the store that's most helpful, or the one who sells the best product, or the one who offers the best solution, or the one who provides the best service, then you will be much more effective with the prospect who wants to shop for price.

6. Closing Power - How many trips to that store will you make before plopping down your money, your check, or your credit card? _____ If you think things over prior to buying, then you will be very vulnerable to the prospect who wants to think about it.

35

"Selling is a self fulfilling prophecy. You will consistently get your prospects to behave in a manner which is consistent with how you would behave, or how you expect your prospect to behave in this situation."

Dave Kurlan

Your problem? You understand. Please understand that the only one who will actually be thinking it over is you! If however, you can look at a product and buy it right then and there, then with proper style and bravery, you have the potential to be in closing encounters of the superstar kind.

7. Customer Loyalty - Do you continue buying from the same store on a regular basis?_____. If you are the loyal customer of a store you deal with, chances are you will have a loyal following yourself. On the other hand, if you buy from different vendors or stores all of the time, you will find yourself with customers who do the same to you. Your problem? You understand.

8. Referral Potential - Do you give quality referrals to salespeople? If you do, you have probably developed a strong referral base, eliminating the need for endless cold calls. On the other hand, I'm sure that you're desperate for quality referrals if you neglect to take care of the salespeople from whom you buy. Your problem? You understand.

9. Sob Story Vulnerability - Is money tight for you? Your prospect tells you that they want what you have, but they just don't have the money. They say that money has really been tight. If that sounds familiar to you, you're vulnerable to that stall. Your problem? You understand.

10. Killer Instinct - Will you find a way to pay for something you want even if you don't have the money? If you will then the chances are good that you expect your prospect to do the same thing. On the other hand if you always wait until the money is there, you'll allow your prospect to do the same. Your problem? You understand.

I'll tell you a story about Steve, a young mortgage originator who came to me for help a while back. Steve said that his last major purchase was a diamond engagement ring for his fiancée'. It cost $1100, took him thirteen months to buy it, and brought him to twenty-seven different stores. He was searching for the lowest price, didn't believe in financing, and made six trips back to the store he finally bought from. A major purchase for Steve was anything more than $50, and Steve sold mortgages for a bank.

When he came to me, he had just finished a terrible year in which he earned merely $3500. He didn't understand why he was failing, and he hoped I could make a difference. I couldn't, and I'll show you why.

If we were to put Steve in front of his typical prospects, the setting would be a young couple's living room, where they are about to finance their first home. You can already see one of the problems here, as Steve doesn't believe in financing. He pays cash for everything!

Steve moves through the sales call as he always does and comes to the close, one I'm sure was pretty weak. His prospects say, "Steve, you're the first person we've spoken to....we really need to see what else is out there."

Well, so wouldn't Steve, to the tune of twenty-seven others. He could have fifty great techniques for handling the "we want to shop around" objection, but he won't use them because he understands. That's what he would do to. What bonding!

Maybe they say, "Steve, you quoted us a rate of 8.5%, but we saw an ad in today's paper for 8.25% at ABC Mortgage Company. We always go with the best price."

Dead Again! Steve would too, even if it took thirteen months to find it! This is yet another example of a situation where the salesperson could have umpteen techniques for handling a price objection, but won't use any of them effectively, or at all, because they understand.

Perhaps the prospects tell Steve, "We never make a decision the first time we see anything!"

Does Steve spring into action here? No. Steve wouldn't make a decision the first time either. Or the second time, the third time, or the fourth time. Steve can't make decisions, so how in the world will he get others to make them? He won't. More powerful techniques go unused!

Here's a good one. The couple says, "You know, we always pay cash for everything, we don't really like payments, we only got credit cards to build our credit so that we'd be able to get a mortgage, but we don't even use them. We're really uncomfortable signing our lives away for thirty years!"

As you know, Steve doesn't believe in financing either, so what's he even doing in this business? My point exactly!

Here's one more he can't handle. "Gee Steve, this is really a lot of money!" It's only $69,950 more than a lot of money to Steve!

Steve was failing miserably in this business because he shouldn't have been there in the first place! His Buy Cycle is totally non-supportive to his sell cycle, resulting in repeated failures. With a Buy Cycle like Steve's, he shouldn't even be in sales. Remember that the Buy Cycle is only one of several dozens records in your Record Collection. It just happens to be the most significant.

If Steve's Buy Cycle is awful and self-limiting, then what would be considered an empowering Buy Cycle for a successful career in sales? Let me share a story of an attempt by my wife and I to buy a television.

Debbie and I finished dinner on a recent summer evening and without more than five minutes of conversation, we decided to buy one of those home theatre, large screen projection televisions. We agreed, based on the vast selection we knew they had, that we'd go to one particular major department store about 30 minutes from our home.

Debbie has become quite a salesperson in her own right. To compliment the superior selling skills she developed over the last five years, she simply goes to the predetermined store, finds what she's looking for in her budget, and just buys it. No shopping from one store to another, no price hunting, no thinking it over, she just buys it.

We arrived at the store about ten minutes prior to closing time. That is the time when the store closes as well as the time it should have taken the salesperson to close us. We quickly selected the model we wanted and were ready to arrange for delivery (or could we take it home with us?). No longer than it takes to say "sold", the salesperson talked us out of the TV that we were ready to pay for, and into another model that he preferred. He had no idea when they could deliver it, we weren't in love with it, and it was beyond the budget we had set for ourselves. So instead of leaving the store excited, in anticipation of our comfortable family room being transformed into a mini movie theatre, we left disappointed, and we vowed never to return because of their incompetence.

During the long ride home we reasoned that we might as well wait until the fall, but we both knew we would be right back out there trying to buy our home theatre unit on Saturday, despite our busy schedule. Much to our happiness, Saturday arrived the very next morning! We put our buying faces on and once again tried to buy a television. This time we would be prepared! We made note of another store we could visit just in case the first store couldn't deliver in time. Clearly it was delivery which would make this sale, rather than who had the best price. Despite that strategy, the salesperson at our first stop didn't realize that we were delivery shopping, and incorrectly assumed we were price shopping. I knew we'd leave this store laughing when, as we walked in he greeted us b(u)y saying, "Welcome to ABC. It's nice to have you here today!" Always being one to respond in the moment and on cue I replied, "Well thanks for having us. It's really s(w)ell to be here!" He laughed when he realized he sounded like a jackass.

After a whirlwind five-minute tour around the televisions, we announced that we were leaving because we had seen this 46" Such and Such over at XYZ that we liked, and they didn't have anything comparable in the same price range. Well it didn't take more than a minute for this salesperson to drop his price by $400 to make a TV fit the price range of the first TV we mentioned. We told him we appreciated his gesture, but we were concerned about delivery. How soon could we have it? He checked and determined that we could get delivery on Tuesday. We asked if it would be possible to get delivery after 5pm because it was the only time we could be home. He checked, and said yes. Since we were so concerned about

"Success comes in cans, failure in cant's."

Elizabeth Taylor

whether they would deliver as promised, as I began to write the check he was nice enough to suggest that we take delivery C.O.D. to assure that we didn't pay for something we wouldn't get. This was getting to be too much. This salesperson didn't talk me out of a television; he talked me out of paying for it!

Well you probably know what happens next. Yes, they called on Monday and confirmed a delivery for Tuesday evening after 5pm. They called again on Tuesday at 3:30 to let us know that their delivery people were already at our home and since we weren't there, they would be unable to deliver the television to us at this time.

I called the store and spoke to the manager, who wasn't able to turn the truck around. He was really good at making excuses. The union, the drivers (didn't have a watch or couldn't read their watch, or didn't see the instructions?), no trucks, no profit, etc. I told him that I didn't call to be given excuses, I called to get our television. He asked what he could do to solve the problem. I told him to find some way, any way, to get our television delivered this evening. I suggested that if it were my store and something like this happened, I would get in the truck myself and get the TV delivered to keep my customer happy. He had more excuses and suggested a Friday delivery. I mentioned that if he took care of us, I'd let everyone know (he obviously had no idea how many people everyone encompassed) that he went out of his way to make us happy. On the other hand, I told Moses (yes, that was the store manager's name) that even more people would know about it if he didn't find a way to do what we had contracted with Fretter of Auburn MA. to do - deliver my television on Tuesday after 5pm.

So once again the store didn't have our money, and we didn't have our home theater unit and I was getting very frustrated at our lack of success. While I was well aware of the ineptitude of most salespeople in America from the tens of thousands I have trained, I was surprised that it could get this bad. Remember, we weren't fighting, giving objections, looking for a better price, or resisting a close. We were trying to buy this television!

Tuesday evening we were at it again following dinner. At this store, we had to wait ten minutes before being helped, at which time the owners son, who didn't feel like helping us, told us we'd be better off with a large television (which happened to be on close out - do you think he was trying to unload them?) instead of a home theater unit. Just what we wanted! So glad he could redirect us! He sensed our frustration and pawned us off on a salesperson, who picking up on my subtle hints as to what he should do (I told him everything that had happened up to this point) only once showed us anything out of our price range, didn't suggest something different than what we wanted, and arranged for our delivery in just fifteen minutes. Why did it take so long?

If you really want to be a champion in the world of sales, a world filled with under trained, very mediocre salespeople, then I suggest that you adopt the microwave buy cycle, the one practiced by most of the country's top salespeople.

Before leaving your house, determine exactly what you want this product to do for you. Forget about features! They'll only confuse things for you. What do you want it to do? Next, decide how much you're willing to spend. It doesn't matter how much they sell for. What are you willing to pay for what you want? Third. Decide upon whom you would like to buy it from. Where have you had the most success in the past, or who would have the best selection, or who would provide the best advice, or who would offer the most reliable service?

You're done! Now, drive to the store, find a competent salesperson, and tell him what you want this product to do and in what price range it must be. Let him suggest which brand or model would satisfy your needs, something he should be able to do once you've told him what your needs are. Of course, if you play games and you aren't straight with him, he'll be useless! After he shows you the unit he believes will solve your problem, you must do one of two things. If you love it and it's what you need, and if it's in your budget, buy it! If you don't love it, or if it's not in your budget, thank him for his time, tell him "no" and go to the store that would be your second choice. DO NOT SAY, "OK, thanks, we're gonna look around and we'll probably be back later." NO "THINK IT OVERS!"

CATCHY TUNES AND THE SALES CALL OF DOOM
6

"I often find that the reason a salesperson is unable to reach a desired outcome is more often the result of a self limiting belief, than a lack of appropriate techniques."

Dave Kurlan

If a salesperson came to me and asked for six killer techniques for handling objections when prospects won't disclose their budget, here's what would probably happen.

He'll go back in the field tomorrow, get in front of a new prospect, ask what their budget is, and then hear one of the following lines: "Don't worry, the money's there." Where is there? And don't you know that "there" is where it will stay? You aren't getting any of it! Or the prospect might say, "hey, money's no object!" Money's never an object when the prospect doesn't plan on spending any of it! Or the prospect might say, "We have a budget, but it's not fair to the other salespeople if we share it with you." Who says we have to be fair? For crying out loud! Here's another one. They say, "There's a budget, but I don't know what it is. It's not my department." Or, how about, "We have no idea what something like this should cost. We were hoping you'd tell us!"

So our salesperson takes out his six new techniques and tries them, only to get more of the same...no budget. So what went wrong? Nothing really. We took a salesperson, Ed, who couldn't uncover a budget yesterday, and we didn't really change him. The only thing we changed were the words coming out of his mouth. And even the words weren't all that different. They were merely different from what he may have normally said in a money situation. All of the techniques in the world won't help, until we change the

Collection of records playing in the background of the salesperson's mind. Ed may have been brought up in a family where it was not polite to talk about money. Maybe there wasn't much

43

money when Ed was growing up. Maybe he was told that it wasn't any of his business. For whatever reasons he may have been uncomfortable talking about money, Ed would not successfully use a technique until he changed his level of comfort with regard to that particular subject.

"It isn't polite to talk about other people's money" is just one self limiting record out of a collection of what could be dozens of self limiting records.

I've listed several dozen of the most "popular" records that I consider to be self-limiting.

1. I have to call on a purchasing agent.
2. I can't call on a company president.
3. I can not close on the first call.
4. I can't shorten my sell cycle.
5. My prospects will only buy if I have the lowest price.
6. It's OK if my prospects wish to shop around.
7. I should educate my prospects.
8. It's OK if my prospects wish to think things over.
9. Prospects who think things over will eventually buy from me.
10. It's important that my prospects like me.
11. The economy is down and my prospects don't have much money.
12. Don't talk to strangers.
13. It's impolite to ask people about their finances.
14. Most prospects are truthful.
15. Most prospects are sincere.
16. I can't sell without literature.
17. I can't sell without first demonstrating my product.
18. I can't confront a prospect.
19. I can't ask a question that might cause my prospect to become upset.
20. I usually think things over before making a decision.
21. I usually look for the lowest price.
22. I need to comparison shop.

23. I do my research before making a major purchase.
24. Money is tight.
25. A major purchase is anything over $150.
26. I need to show my prospect that I know what I'm talking about.
27. My customers won't give me referrals.
28. My business is different.
29. My product is more difficult to sell.
30. Some of the concepts in this book don't apply to me.
31. Some prospects are really difficult.
32. Questions might cause my prospect to become upset.
33. There are certain things that you just can't say.
34. I have to answer the questions that a secretary may ask of me.
35. I'm doing OK.
36. It's normal to get objections on a sales call.
37. You can't change bid specs after the RFP (request for proposal) has been issued.
38. Money isn't that important to me.
39. My product or service costs a lot of money.
40. I have a long sell cycle.
41. If they're happy with their current vendor I can't sell to them.
42. It's rude to ask a lot of questions.
43. I'm not happy with who I am.
44. I must dominate the conversation.
45. I don't like cold calls.
46. I can't fake sincerity.
47. If I'm right and the prospect is wrong I must correct them.
48. I don't have time to prospect.
49. My territory is the most difficult in which to sell.
50. The most important part of the sales call is the quote.
51. The most important part of the sales call is the presentation.
52. The most important part of the sales call is making friends.
53. Don't talk to strangers.
54. I can't ask a question that might upset a prospect.
55. A negative prospect is the toughest to sell.

"You can have a stack of the newest, most powerful techniques ever created and if the intended outcome or the technique itself is in contradiction to your beliefs, you will misdeliver the move or shy away from the situation altogether."

Dave Kurlan

56. The government must go with the lowest bid.

I often find that the reason a salesperson is unable to reach a desired outcome is more often the result of a self-limiting belief, than the lack of an available appropriate technique. These self-limiting beliefs, or records, play out in our heads automatically, just like your favorite songs. Have you ever found yourself humming, whistling, or singing a song that you're fond of, only to wonder why, how and when you started? With your self limiting collection of records, and the collection of supportive records as well, you can actually listen in on the process of self programming. What your records contain will determine the way you will perform on your sales calls. You can possess a stack of the newest, most powerful, techniques ever created and if the intended outcome or the technique itself is in contradiction to your record, you will probably misdeliver the move, or shy away from the situation altogether.

Make a list of those self-limiting records that you possess, and along side of each record, write down the outcomes that you get as a result of the self-limiting record. Next, write down the approximate amount of additional business you may have written during the last twelve months, had you not been burdened with these self-limiting records. Calculate the commissions you would have earned from all of that additional business. Now multiply this total by the number of years that you've been in sales. You have just calculated the value of your record collection, not only its worth, but the amount of money it has prevented you from earning up until now!

For each and every one of your self-limiting records, write down how you would like those outcomes to change, if you actually had the ability to change them. Next, you'll need to rewrite the records

"The only problem with winning the low bid is that.... when it's all said and done you've lost money."

Dave Kurlan

until they are worded in such a way that they will bring a profitable outcome to your sales calls. Make sure that they all read as positive affirmations. They should not begin with I can't, I won't, I will not, or anything else negative. They must all begin with I will, I must, I can, I have, I am, or I do.

Next you can record these new affirmations on a sixty-minute tape. In your own voice, read each supportive record. When you've completed reading the set, start over and continue reading the set of supportive records, over and over, until the entire 60 minute tape has been filled. Play this tape in your car, between sales calls, when you're asleep at night, and anywhere else you can, until you're "singing" these new, empowering, positive records automatically. When you've reached the point where you can't get these records out of you head, the reprogramming has been completed!

My first business was a specialty shop. We sold high end musical instruments. I learned many lessons during my ten years of ownership, but two record collection stories stand out in my mind.

Paul, who would later become my partner, was new to selling, having just graduated from college. He had been struggling to make sales for a couple of weeks when I took a phone call from a lady who was looking for a nice guitar for her daughter. Over the phone, we determined that $200 would allow her to buy a good quality, yet inexpensive first guitar. She said she'd be in around 2pm that afternoon. In an attempt to help Paul become comfortable with just making a sale, I told him that a nice lady would drop in at 2pm to pick out a guitar for her daughter, and that it was already sold.

This was very important for me to convey, since his biggest problem had been determining whether someone was ready to buy, and then getting the sale closed. After two weeks of misfires, bad timing, and failures, his lack of success was threatening to destroy his confidence.

47

"A "no" uttered from the deepest conviction is better and greater than a "yes" merely uttered to please, or what is worse, to avoid trouble."

Mahatma Ghandhi

As scheduled, a nice lady walked in the store at 2pm and told him she was looking for a guitar for her daughter. While he failed to properly question her as to need, or budget, he did go right for that $200 guitar, put it in a case, and write up a slip.

You're probably asking what the big deal is, and rightly so. It sounded pretty easy, especially since it was already set up. The incredible part of this story is that this was not the lady I spoke to on the phone earlier in the day. This lady just happened to come in at the right time, just happened to be looking for a guitar, and just happened to be looking for her daughter. He could have shown her several...and confused her. He could have shown her guitars for less money...and left money on the table. He could have shown her several guitars for more money, but he wouldn't have, because he wouldn't have spent more than $200 for a guitar himself! Since he was fooled into believing that this was the lady who was already closed, she was easily closed because Paul was finally comfortable being in this situation!

Paul never had a problem closing after that, and as a matter of fact, he became a superior closer. He learned that if you believed that you would have difficulty closing a prospect, you most certainly would. He found that whenever he believed he could easily close anyone and everyone, he usually did.

We did a lot of business with school systems, mostly through bids. It was widely believed that once the bid requests were sent out, there wasn't much you could do except bid and hope you had the lowest price. The only problem with winning the low bid is that you never make any money, and in the case of the government, you wait forever to get paid, which means that when it's all said and done you've probably lost money, unless the contract was so large that even a small percentage of profit could add up to something substantial.

I didn't subscribe to that line of thinking - I believed then, and still believe now that the originator of the bid could be contacted. They could be asked questions about the specifications, as well as their reasons for choosing the product or the brand they specified. If there was a better product to solve their problem than the one requested it was often possible to bid on the superior solution. The catch was that you or I would be the only one bidding on the revised solution, because we got the specs changed after the requests for bids went out, and it would be more profitable than on that which everyone else would be bidding. Furthermore, the prospect would be on the look out for my bid, remembering our phone conversation, as well as my superior solution.

Just a couple of weeks ago Debbie (remember my wife?) demonstrated the practicality of this theory. Using the philosophy I described before, Debbie was awarded a contract with the state for four times the amount of the next lowest bidder.

Do you remember the expression "I'll believe it when I see it?" Dr. Wayne Dyer wrote a book he titled "I'll See It When I Believe It." This is clearly the way you must think if you are to succeed in sales.

The music of selling may be the most critical element of success. Your supportive record collection will support any effective technique. A self-limiting collection will keep all effective techniques from working.

THE STAMP OF APPROVAL

7

"Need for approval goes largely unnoticed by the salesperson and his sales manager."

Dave Kurlan

I would be willing to bet that more than 90% of all salespeople have what the psychologists call need for approval. My problem is that it's not really a psychological problem, it's a societal problem. Peer pressures and need for approval go hand in hand. From as early as preschool, children are encouraged to make friends. Teenagers live in hopes of being popular. When an individual gets his first job, he's urged to get his boss to like him. Without this peer pressure and need for approval, students, not driven to academic success, would fail their classes and drop out of school. On the positive side, more youngsters would continue their pursuit of such uncool hobbies as dance, art, music, and tennis, without the fear of being snubbed by their classmates. This phenomenon takes place primarily in America. As anyone who has negotiated with a Middle Easterner would tell you, their motives are to get what they want, not to please people. Unfortunately, people cite their love of people as the number one reason for joining the ranks of salespeople. Money is the number two reason, but there are problems with that which I'll explore in an upcoming chapter.

Need for Approval is largely unnoticed by the salesperson and the sales manager. Some sales trainers are capable of picking this problem up, but most salespeople have limited exposure to professional trainers, likely attending less than one seminar every couple of years. Even when they do choose to attend sales training, it's usually of the "100 techniques" variety and not the kind where serious problems are addressed and solved.

While it is usually hidden to its owner, need for approval accounts for at least 30% of the sales that slip through their fingers, either to a competitor or to the uncommitted prospect that just never gets off the dime. Killer instinct, if the salesperson has it, will often be neutralized here. Many salespeople played competitive sports and had tremendous killer instinct in their given sport, yet because of their strong need for approval, are unable to use it in selling situations.

There are several more important skills that are often neutralized by the need for approval. First and most important are questions. While need for approval won't prevent you from asking questions, it will usually keep you from asking the tough ones. Suppose we have a prospect who isn't quite where we need him to be in order for us to feel reasonably comfortable about there being business for us. We've found that he needs our product or service but may not have admitted to having a problem - either to himself or to us. He's happy with his present vendor, doesn't wish to change, has been with them for a long time, but he hinted that there might be some problems. The real challenge is that he isn't calling them problems, we are. He seems to think the shortcomings of his supplier are OK. All it will take to get him where we want him is one question. A tough question.

A risky question. A question that could get the prospect upset. A question which could bring the business our way. We have to ask something like, "have you lowered your expectations, or have you always accepted mediocrity?"

The only problem with that is, when you have need for approval, you can't ask a question if there's a risk that your prospect will get upset. As a result, instead of getting a chance to turn this prospect around, creating a chance to do business, we'll call on this prospect four times a year for the next five years, wasting hours of time, wondering why we can't get this person to change suppliers!

What if we had a prospect that was lying to us? This is interesting because in most cases salespeople aren't even aware of the lies. This happens because so many salespeople have an overly idealistic view of people, who upon becoming prospects, change dramatically. While people in general could be expected to show

51

"I don't know the key to success, but the key to failure is trying to please everybody."

Bill Cosby

honesty, integrity and courtesy, prospects are usually quite the opposite. It's actually ironic that people think salespeople are liars, when in reality, most salespeople are more honest, sometimes too honest, compared to their prospects! Until we learn to swallow that truth, we'll be blind-sided time after time. Let's pretend that we recognize the lies this time. The situation calls for a confrontation; one that most salespeople can't pull off for fear that the prospect will get upset. Of course if the prospect is lying then it should be obvious that there isn't any business for you if you don't confront!

People with need for approval are notorious for their inability to confront. It should be noted that a confrontation doesn't have to be nasty, and in fact, normally isn't. A salesperson who wishes to be successful in sales must learn to confront, which often begins with a non threatening question like, "can I say something without getting you upset?" or, "can I ask you a question without it sounding like a confrontation?" When you read my chapter on sports, games, fun and war you may get a different slant on selling, one which may help you to overcome your need for approval.

The ability to close the sale is most crucial in selling. If you can't close at your first opportunity, and do it consistently, anything else you've accomplished along the way matters! Closing at the first opportunity does not necessarily mean closing on the first call, although it could. There is always a "first" opportunity, and the first is always the best. The first opportunity comes when the prospect is finally closable. You've developed some bonding and rapport, they've agreed that they need it, they're committed to solving their problem, they can afford it, you're talking with someone who's able to make a decision, they've agreed to make a decision, and you have the best solution for their problem, and within their budget. When you've reached the point in the process where all of those pieces have been put together, you have your first closing opportunity. If you don't close at the first opportunity, your chances decrease in proportion to the amount of time that has passed since you let the opportunity slip through your fingers. For the approval seekers, this is probably the part of process where they will most easily recognize themselves. Many salespeople with need for approval love people. This fondness often translates into their having good people skills, good personalities, and pride in their knowledge of their product or service. As a result, it isn't uncommon for them to hear just how wonderful they are after they attempt their first close. It sounds like, "Gee, Tom, we really like you. You're not like the others. You've been real helpful to us. We learned a lot! There's a good chance that we'll be doing business!"

Now this is exactly what the stroke deprived, approval-seeking salesperson wants to hear. Unfortunately, the prospect has learned that a mega-stroke will usually prove to be a very effective put-off. Time after time, the prospect has smartly and subtly placed a put-off after a mega-stroke and watched salespeople retreat to their office. The salesperson, hearing what he needed to hear and suddenly aware of how much the prospect "likes him", won't say anything which could upset the apple cart. No pressure, no tough questions, no techniques, no second efforts, and no chance to get the business. Need for approval helps to determine whether the salesperson can shorten or lengthen his cycle.

We've discussed how need for approval keeps salespeople from asking tough questions, from confronting, and from closing when there is resistance in the form of a put off. These same problems keep salespeople from getting appointments by phone when they are unable to navigate beyond the put offs. So they don't get in front of enough prospects, and they aren't effective closing those they do see. If you have need for approval you're also liable to be thrown off track by people who need your help. Since you're liable to have trouble saying "no" to people, you'll help them out at the expense of your own performance.

When you have trouble saying "no" to people, you're in for additional difficulties on your sales calls as well. When prospects tell you things like "looks good", or "there's a good chance", you won't have an opportunity to find out why they aren't buying because they're telling you that they will buy, but not today. One of the more effective tactics used by winning salespeople is the negative sell, a facet of which is to make a difficult prospect say "no". When you get your prospect to say no, you'll finally have an opportunity to learn why they haven't committed to a purchase. Then you can begin to sell again.

The problem we're faced with here is that when you have this much trouble saying no to people, you'll find it even more difficult to make them say no. You may be just as uncomfortable hearing that word as you are saying it, thereby neutralizing the approach. Once again you're in a situation where your need for approval prevents you from being effective.

Gary had acute need for approval when he came to me for coaching. He was a fifteen-year veteran of the insurance industry and was successful by insurance standards, but hardly living up to expectations according to mine.

The insurance industry is it's own worst enemy when it comes to developing salespeople. It's an industry, much like the real estate industry, where mediocrity is applauded and failure is accepted. It's also an industry where a salesperson with a good work ethic, a minimum of self limiting records in his collection, and fair style will earn over $150,000 after several years in the business.

Gary had been performing at a level that allowed his boss to earn some decent over ride commissions, and that paid most of Gary's substantial bills. While Gary had long suspected that he could be doing much better, his boss continued to applaud his mediocrity, even helping him to win trips and honors by giving him credit for business which he didn't write.

Gary was a good example of someone who after fifteen years in sales had some sales know how, could have used some more, but even with more skills, wouldn't have been able to execute because of his need for approval. He had one particular fear that was quite unusual. Gary had been doing all of his business for fifteen years without benefit of referrals or add on business because his need for approval kept him from returning to his existing clients, for fear that they would not welcome him back.

On the bright side we had a salesperson that despite his tenure would continue to make cold calls and write new business. On the dark side, he had an untapped client base and was depriving himself of virtually every benefit his fifteen years in the business could bring. Of equal concern was the fact that since he did not choose to return to his clients after selling them, they were ripe to be plucked by even a mildly aggressive competitor.

On the calls Gary did initiate, he was plagued by stalls, put-offs, lies, objections, and he invested a myriad of wasted time with prospects who would not be doing business with him. Some of the reasons for his frustration could be linked to skill, but most had to be attributed to his need for approval. He couldn't confront a lying prospect if his life depended on it. He couldn't ask a tough question even if a positive outcome were guaranteed. He couldn't have an in-depth conversation about their finances because he was afraid they'd become upset. All of these limitations caused him to remain very emotionally involved, most of the time. He rarely had any control, rarely knew what would happen next, and most often, his hunches that prospects were going to purchase turned out to be wrong.

As a result, Gary worked too hard, and had little to show for it. He became discouraged and frustrated, and developed a severe self-limiting record titled "I'm not good enough." The latter devastated his self-image. With low self-esteem, a salesperson rarely feels "up" to doing his prospecting, waging battle with a difficult prospect, or making changes to better himself. So Gary sank to new depths.

As a rule it often takes four to eight months to coach a salesperson out from under his need for approval. If the problem is compounded with low self-esteem as well, it will take even longer, because the need for approval can not be effectively overcome until self-image has been improved. When the salesperson is finally feeling good about himself again, feeling stronger, and readies himself for coping with his weaknesses, we can begin to work on a major weakness like the need for approval.

What I attempt to do first for a salesperson with need for approval is to accomplish an intermediate step. Respect works fairly well here. It is important for the prospect to respect the salesperson, especially the salesperson that calls on businesses for a living. I'll give you an example. Suppose you own a business and you're shopping for commercial insurance. You must have this coverage, so it's not a matter of whether you'll buy as much as it's a question of who you'll do business with. You've been around long enough to know that cheapest doesn't mean best solution, but you're bluffing with the salesperson that is currently in front of you. You tell him that you can get the same policy for 20% less from someone else and that you expect him to sharpen his pencil. You know he has the policy that will give you the needed coverage, but you're trying to get it for a little less. The policy you're bluffing against is significantly less, but offers little in the way of coverage. You can be closed right now, but the salesperson wimps out instead, says he'll get back to you, and heads back for his office.

In the mean time, you call another agent and work a deal with him instead. When you call on business owners the bottom line remains the same. It's not price, rather it's the following: If a crisis were to occur in eight months and you need someone to take care of you right then and there, when push comes to shove, is this particular salesperson capable of standing up to his company and making something happen on your behalf?

While the wimp with need for approval is nice enough, and is liked well enough by the business owner, he is not respected, not viewed as a problem solver, and not perceived as someone who could be counted on in a time of need. So who is it that is perceived to be the person that can be relied upon? Who could stand up to his company? Who could take charge in a crisis? Who will get the respect of this prospect? Someone with the guts to confront. Someone with the confidence to ask the tough questions. Someone with the self-respect to call a prospect on a bluff.

So it's not approval that will cause a prospect to do business, rather, it's respect. Approval seeking will make friends. Respect seeking will make you money. Once you decide which perception you'd like to create, the rest is programming, practicing, and repetition.

Dr. Wayne Dyer wrote an earlier book entitled "Your Erroneous Zones", in which he devotes several wonderful pages to overcoming the need for approval. Dan Millman, in his book, No Ordinary Moments, also gives some wonderful advice with regard to need for approval.

SPORTS, GAMES, AND WAR
8

"What would happen if Eckersley had need for approval? He would be worried about what Carlton Fisk might think of him if Dennis were to make him look bad. Not wishing to jeopardize a friendship, Dennis might make a different pitch than he normally would have, allowing Fisk to hit a tremendous two run homer to win the game."

After we have achieved a minimal understanding that respect is more important than approval, we can move to the next level, one where we can distinguish between people and prospects. Most people are sincere, trustworthy, straight, well intentioned, and loyal. Most prospects possess none of those attributes. The problem is that prospects look like people, act like people, sound like people, and appear to be people. Unfortunately, they aren't people any more than wolves could be the house pets that Golden Retrievers tend to be.

Salespeople are people too, and as salespeople you must do things that you wouldn't necessarily be comfortable doing as socially. The tough questions, the confrontations, the pressure, and the strategies may all be inappropriate for social situations, but they are very appropriate for selling.

As an example, let's take a three hundred-pound tackle on a pro football team. Each and every Sunday, he's expected to trot out to that line of scrimmage, maneuver himself into that familiar, but uncomfortable looking squat, and knock grown men to the ground. Not with a little push mind you, but with a diving, head on frontal attack! And he gets paid for this, applauded by tens of thousands of fans, admired by millions of TV viewers, and fanny patted by his teammates! His mother even approves! But what would happen if he were to walk on the sidewalk in downtown Dallas TX, and for no reason at all, tackle a sweet old lady, or an innocent little girl, or for that matter, a tough looking biker on his Harley Davidson?

"Let us never negotiate out of fear, but let us never fear to negotiate."

John F. Kennedy

Handcuffs, jail, bail, trial, shame, suspension, bankruptcy, and eventually, gone and forgotten, a lonely death.

It's OK that we do the things we do in sales, as long as we don't do the things we do in sales when we're not selling! Let me introduce some words that have nothing to do with closing, but which even salespeople associate with the process. Pressure, arm wrestling, deceit, lying, fast talking, pushy, nasty, aggressive, obnoxious, sweet, accommodating, overly patient, too impatient, empathetic, and rude.

I see great many similarities between sales, sports, and board games, and in some situations, war! The finest attribute a salesperson can possess is his ability to close. In 1992 Dennis Eckersley, of the Oakland Athletics won the American League's Cy Young Award. He was only the third relief pitcher in history to win this coveted award. If you look up "closer" in the baseball encyclopedia, you'll find Dennis' picture! What made him such a good closer? You'll find that many of the characteristics that make a baseball closer great are common to the great sales closer. They include tremendous concentration, great killer instinct, experience, total control of their emotions, yet **"Let us** incredible passion for that which they are doing, endless practice, tremendous confidence, strong self worth, and absolutely no need for approval. Suppose one of Dennis' friends came to the plate for the Chicago White Sox, with two outs in the bottom of the ninth inning and Oakland leading by one run. What would happen if Eckersley had need for approval? He would be worried about what Carlton Fisk might think of him if Dennis were to make him look bad. Not wishing to jeopardize a friendship, Dennis might make a different pitch than he normally would have, allowing Fisk to hit a tremendous two run homer to win the game. But Eckersley doesn't have need for approval!

If you've ever played any tennis, you know what it feels like to hit a nice, strong, forcing ground stroke deep into the back hand corner of your opponent, and as you charge the net he pops a short, weak lob to your forehand side. You glide underneath the ball, set yourself, and get ready to pound the ever-living hell out of the ball! You don't worry about what your opponent might think of you, because it's a game, and like most sports, it's played to win, it's played for fun, and it has its own set of rules.

In order to win in sports you must execute, you must compete, you must have the desire to win, you shouldn't become inventive, you have to work within the rules of the sport, you ought to have fun, and you must not think. Just work the system.

In order to win at games, you must execute, you must compete, you must have the desire to win, you shouldn't become inventive, you have to work within the rules of the game, you ought to have fun, and you're asked to think. Just play the game.

In war, to win you must execute, you must compete, you must have the desire to stay alive, you shouldn't become inventive, you have to work within the rules of the Geneva Convention, you should try to have fun, and you must not think. The only difference with war is that it's a life or death situation at all times. Sport imitates war on the football field, the basketball court and the hockey rink during the final two minutes of competition, when the game often becomes a veritable battle. The athlete, who must perform in order to have his contract renewed for one more season, or to increase his worth in the free agent market, is fighting for his right to earn a living in his chosen field.

To win in sales you must execute, you shouldn't become inventive, you have to work within the rules of selling, you must have fun but don't think so much. You will have battles that resemble the final two minutes of a ball game. You will have moments where you are fighting to earn a living in your chosen profession. You will have to take your prospect down to the mat when faced with a sell or starve situation. You will have to fight for your life in a very competitive world.

There really isn't much of a difference between sports, games, war and selling. Since we're talking about selling let's write the rules.

On every sales call you're fighting for your right to earn a living.

All prospects are going to lie to you about something.

You must be in total control of every selling situation, each and every step of the way.

Your prospect should never know that you're in control.

It doesn't matter what anyone thinks or says about you as long as they do think and talk about you.

Selling is a sport so play to win.

Selling is a science so you must use a systematic approach.

Selling is a game so have fun.

Selling is a profession so it's best to make a lot of money at it.

Selling is an art so prepare for the road to mastery.

Selling is like music so learn to read the sheet music.

There is no luck in selling, just skill.

A good personality will help you to make friends, not money.

A technical approach will make you knowledgeable, but not necessarily effective.

Strong desire and commitment = effort.

Consistent effort over time will produce results.

Selling has its moments so you must become rejection proof.

Selling has its bad times so you must become failure proof.

Selling has its rewards so you must predefine them.

Selling requires good instincts, and they must be developed over time.

It will take at least 750 hours of face to face selling to learn these lessons.

There's no such thing as an objection.

Invest your money in acting lessons.

Practice thirty minutes each day.

Flexibility translates into earning power.

Leave your ego in the car.

"Honest differences are often a healthy sign of progress."

Mahatma Ghandhi

Those things that are most uncomfortable for you to do are the very things you are here to overcome.

If you wait until you're comfortable, you'll be waiting a very long time.

That which is most uncomfortable for you may be very comfortable for your prospect.

That which is most comfortable for you may just anger your prospect to the point of not doing business.

During your career in sales there will be three kinds of sales calls. The easy ones are there for the taking, so take them. The difficult ones may require you to do some things that you may find uncomfortable. So take a deep breath and learn to be comfortable. The "for experts only" sales calls will absolutely require you to do things which both you and your prospect may will find uncomfortable. Do them anyway.

It's much easier for a baseball hitter to face the likes of the soft throwing Mike Boddicker, he of the 80 mph fast ball, than someone like Rocket Roger Clemens with his 95 mph fast ball. None the less, a professional baseball player will gear up to be just a little bit quicker, concentrate more, have more intensity, and rise to the challenge brought on when facing a "tough customer"

As a professional salesperson you will repeatedly be in pressure packed, crucial situations which call for your experience, your skill, your desire to win, your love of a good time, your love for a challenge, and your killer instinct. The only thing which could get in the way is you, with a low self image, a self limiting record collection, a fear of failure, a need for approval and an inability to control your emotions. Fortunately, you have control over all of these things, if you want the control.

GREENBACKS

9

"Money is like an arm or a leg - use it or lose it."

Henry Ford

They say that love makes the world go 'round, and that may be true, but in sales the only thing that makes your world go 'round is money. Salespeople should never leave money on the table in a selling situation. I'm not suggesting that the salesperson overcharge or oversell, rather I make it a hard and fast rule that a salesperson should not under sell and he shouldn't sell for a smaller margin than desired.

In order to accomplish this, the salesperson must be very thorough in his dialogue with the prospect with regard to money. How much he has, how much he'll spend and how he'll spend it are crucial pieces of information which must be uncovered during the selling process. It takes a significant desire for money to become comfortable having conversations of this type. The fact is that because many people do not enter sales to make a lot of money they have an immediate limitation. A lack of motivation for money translates into a lack of desire. A lack of desire allows for a lack of commitment and with these beliefs there is a breakdown in the process of growth and change.

It is better to wish for a lot of money as opposed to a little if you're in a sales career, but it may be in conflict with your life's goals, your values, or your upbringing. I have yet to meet a top-notch salesperson that wasn't also very well off financially.

People have debated the money issue with me for years and while they may actually be right about not needing money, they soon learn that I am right about not becoming successful in sales without the desire for money. Without monetary rewards, it isn't worth the time, the effort, or the pain that you will endure to make changes, overcome failures, and put up with a less than wonderful assortment of prospects you will meet you along the way.

If a lack of money motivation holds you back, then your inability to comfortably talk about money will keep you from getting started! The inability to have an in depth financial conversation with your prospect may cause consistent over quoting, under quoting, and re-quoting. The dropping of prices, lost orders, a longer sell cycle, and regular guesswork will also accompany your discomfort with the money issue.

The successful salesperson always knows, early in the cycle, exactly how much money a prospect will spend to fix their problem, and with him specifically. Additionally, he'll know exactly from where the money is coming. This is quite different from suggesting a dollar amount to your prospect and assuming that your number will be "competitive" or asking them if they have a budget, or how much might be in their budget.

I recently fired one of my individual-coaching clients. Raji had been coming to me for about seven years, and was a model client - that is of what a client shouldn't be. While he had surely grown and improved over seven years, it wasn't the growth we should have seen. He had developed the skills to be earning $200,000 per year, sold the kind of products which would allow him to make that much money, and more than anything else, he had a need to make that much money! Yet here he was, still struggling, never having enough money to live on.

The day I fired him was the turning point in his career. I explained that he had never mustered the level of commitment that was needed to get past his $50,000 per year income. To some of you, there's probably nothing wrong with $50,000, but for Raji, it was living on the edge. He and his wife had five beautiful daughters, all of them smarter than Radji, who was extremely intelligent himself. I reasoned that with two of them already in college, with three more to go, with all of them attending good schools, the tuition alone could cost $60,000 per year when the third daughter comes of age. Then there are men. In the finest colleges, they are bound to

"Blessed is he that expects nothing, for he shall never be disappointed."

Ben Franklin

meet boys from wealthy families who, accustomed to money, will expect big fancy weddings. These would quite possibly cost $50,000 -$100,000 each. Then there was this cloud over his head from the IRS. He had owed them enough money since the 1970's, so that with interest and penalty, his debt had soared to $80,000!

I said, "Radji, it's real obvious that you need to make $200,000 per year, your skills are worth $200,000, and you won't allow yourself to go past $50,000. What is your problem?"

Well, it seems that our Radji was a hippie back in the sixties. The entire hippie movement was anti government, anti establishment, anti capitalism, and mostly anti money. For several years he lived on $40 per week. Obviously, some of this anti materialistic, anti greed, anti money programming was still going very much in place.

On top of this, the IRS called him in each year to discuss his debt, hardly any of that is he ever able to pay. Each year they review his earnings, look at his expenses, look at his debt and stamp "uncollectable" on his folder, writing off several thousand dollars of liability in the process! If he makes more money than he's earning now, the IRS will make him pay his back taxes!

Then there's college. Right now, with his daughter's academic abilities and his lack of money, they're getting an enormous amount of financial aid. If he were to make more money, much of this aid would go away, leaving Radji to foot the bill. He and his wife both live in the least desirable part of a most prestigious, wealth laden town, driving the cars of choice, a ten year old Volvo and a similarly outdated Lynx. What's a Lynx?

His firing came as quite a shock. Here was his mentor, who had always helped, Abandoning him. Or was I? According to the thank you letter I received from Radji, I sent him just the wake up call he needed to realize that he had been depriving his family of the things

65

he and his wife had when they grew up. He was shortchanging himself, by imposing a rule of self suffering and doing without. He had even become a Born Again Christian, carrying around mixed feelings and guilt about making money, whereas, while "Jesus would provide" if they went without, he could tithe an awful lot of money to his church if he became a money maker and he felt he was letting them down as a result.

One of my corporate clients was deep into the fourth quarter of their fiscal year and in need of an additional $1.4 million to meet plan. They were relying on a few big orders to come through so that they would go over the top for the year. Their top salesperson had been working on a deal with a major corporation and according to him and his regional sales manager, it was a done deal. John had submitted a quote for $425 thousand just two months earlier and his manager assured me that the quote was equal to the prospect's budget.

I suggested that in order to get things wrapped up by Christmas they should say something like, "Let's decide whether we want to do business with each other. If we do, we can lock ourselves in a room, sit around a table and work out the details and find a way to get it done. If we don't then we can all move on." They followed my suggestion and John sat at a table for eight hours with representatives from the prospect's company. They worked out all of the details - except for one! Money. Why not money? John incorrectly assumed that money wasn't an issue. When push came to shove however, the prospect, in no hurry to sign a contract, yet acutely aware of John's need to get the deal done by Christmas, played his hand.

The prospect insisted that the price had to come down to $361,000 and not a penny more. How the deal was finally resolved and put to bed is not as important as how the prospect developed the leverage to push my client up against the wall. John, a supposed pro, never determined how much his prospect would spend on his solution. He had learned of the $416 thousand budget, but he failed to learn that only part of that total was ear marked for his part of the solution. Had he learned that on the first or second call, he could

66

have structured the best $361 thousand solution that he could engineer. That's always more desirable than pulling components out of a system at the last minute or dropping the price at the eleventh hour.

There are many explanations for a salesperson's discomfort with jumping headfirst into financial discussions. They may not understand finances to begin with, often the fault of management for not enlightening them. Armed with this knowledge they are at least able to carry on a conversation knowing what to talk about. They may believe that it is none of their business, a self-limiting record for which they will continue to pay a high price. They may feel embarrassed about having to ask the financial questions. Perhaps they wouldn't want someone asking those questions of them. It's possible that in some instances the money they need to talk about is so much to them that they think it to be too much money to discuss with the prospect. In other words, they would never consider spending $50 thousand on anything - even if they had it - so they believe that the prospect wouldn't either.

That brings up another common misunderstanding. Most people believe that other people see the world, behave in life, and interpret situations, and think, exactly as they do. Many trainers teach their trainees that there are four primary types of people, or personalities, and then some combinations of the four. That still only comes to about sixteen! After more than twenty years in sales and probably more than thirty five thousand prospects, I'm sure that there are at least thirty five thousand different types of people! Everyone is different, each with a different way of processing information, a different outlook on life, a different way of looking at things, and an entirely different set of beliefs unique to themselves. Everything in this book consists of my perceptions, my interpretations, my experiences, my beliefs, and my uniqueness. If you agreed with everything I've said, you certainly would not have needed to read it!

Very often you and your prospect will have a different view as to the nature of their problem and what might be the most appropriate solution. If you can get your prospect to agree with and understand the statement, "if you agreed with everything I said today, you wouldn't have needed me to be here...", then you have paved the way for more meaningful dialogue and an eventual sale without arguing over the differing points of view.

TIMELY VISITS

10

"The most beautiful thing we can experience is the mysterious. It is the source of all true art and science."

Albert Einstein

This is my weird chapter, where I can relate the events, people, encounters, and strange phenomenon that in some way had a profound effect on my career, my ability to sell, to train, and ultimately, to write this book. I believe that most people have either had things like these occur them or had the opportunity for things like these to occur, but suppressed them. I'm thankful for the experiences, the consequences, the weirdness, and the general disbelief that people show when I speak of events like these. It keeps them on their toes.

The first significant experience actually paved the way for my entry into sales and only four months later, the second event catapulted me into sales forever. In the summer of '73 I was emotionally immature, younger than my seventeen years, and a terribly naive boy. I was never one to ever touch alcohol drugs and cigarettes throughout my youth and adult life. On one of the rare Saturday evenings where I didn't stay at home alone and watch television, I was out with a friend of mine and two of his drunken friends. I was petrified when the driver, who was intoxicated, ran a stop sign, crossed a busy highway without looking, and entered a one way street heading the wrong way. I saw certain death or dismemberment in my near future, so I invented an excuse to leave the car immediately. I suddenly "remembered" an imaginary job interview that I was to have at the Swim & Tennis Club - that night! Oh God, I couldn't possibly miss it!

They dropped me off, I hitch hiked home, and they got into a car accident. You're probably anticipating that the prophetic part of the incident was my avoiding the car accident, but the real fateful part was the Monday morning phone call I received from the owner of this Swim & Tennis Club! I invented the job interview excuse, but the phone call was real and to make matters even better, I could skip the interview. The job was mine. This was pretty freaky and pretty exciting at the same time. I had planned to spend the summer playing forty hours of tennis per week, not working 80 hours per week at the tennis club. I was in charge of maintenance. I also learned that I had real control of my destiny. If I could at least see or visualize a scenario in my mind's eye then I could get it to happen - perhaps the greatest ability God was to give to me - and to you.

After working for four months I had acquired a taste for earning money, something I believed only happened because I wished for it to happen. This craving paved the way for incident number two. After just two months of college, I was failing miserably, unable to study because I had never learned how. I was thoroughly unhappy and I was always depressed. On the day I decided that I had experienced enough of college and needed something else with which to fill my time, I found a flyer on the windshield of my car which said, "Why Borrow Money? Earn $2.84 per hour - part time. The minimum wage in 1973 was something like $1.75, so the offer was generous, and at the ripe old age of eighteen I was ready to learn what I had to do in order to earn the big bucks!

The interview took place in a one-room office, about 200 square feet with a dirty tile floor. There was a lightweight metal desk in one corner; a folding table at the front of the room, and two rows of folding metal chairs lined up in front of the table. It looked "Mickey Mouse" to me, but what did I really know at that stage of my life? I guessed that it was some sort of sales job, and I knew that I was certainly the least likely candidate on planet Earth for a job selling anything. I was terribly shy, introverted, petrified of people, and unable to carry on a conversation with another person. One of the things I didn't know then, but which I've learned over the last twenty years was that many of the greatest salespeople I have ever known were also introverted, rather than extroverted like so many experts claim.

Being introverted by itself doesn't make anyone automatic material for selling, but when introverted people have strong enough desire for success, and learn how to act extroverted, no one can sell any better. This is because most introverted people don't have any need for approval, having only needed themselves for most of their life. The key is whether they can learn to act extroverted. Those who are naturally extroverted often have so much need for approval that despite their wonderful personality, they often spend most of their selling day needing people to like them, rather than getting people to like them.

The product was quite impressive. Very sharp, very shiny, very high quality, somewhat pizzazzy, and very pricey. Certainly people wouldn't really spend this much money, $165 back in 1973, for a set of ten kitchen knives! It didn't really matter because there was no way in hell that I, with three friends in the whole world, a musician, a tennis player, a wimp - could sell anything to anybody - especially knives! Not even superior knives!

I quickly told Mr. Adamik, the sales manager, that I would not be able to handle this job, under any condition, no matter what, and thanked him for his time. Despite the fact that he would have taken anyone who would fork over the $119 to become an authorized distributor and own their own sample set of cutlery, I'm sure that he knew that I couldn't "cut" it either.

I experienced phenomenon number three as I prepared to leave the building. As I approached the staircase I was forced to turn around and walk back towards the sales manager's office. The force was powerful, but invisible. As I stood in front of him, and to my total amazement, the words "I'll take the job" came rolling out of my mouth! I swear to this day that I'm not the one who made my lips move, but this began an unlikely journey into the world of selling, one which I was very unprepared for at age eighteen.

There were dozens of other strange, unusual, and unexplained events. I'll share those that had an impact on the eventual writing of this book.

First there was David Sandler. Although he and I had our differences later on, he played a major part in my progress. In 1983 I attended a seminar put on by the Sandler Sales Institute. Ron Pisano was the trainer and Paul and I were among the forty attendees. While thirty-nine of the people in the room found something of use during the course of the day, I found the answer to several questions I had been asking for some time.

One question was, "I've been successful selling, but I don't follow any traditional selling rules, so how am I able to do what I do?" I learned that David Sandler had already developed the theory and had a full-fledged selling system to go along with it.

My second question was, "I want to have my own sales training business by 1986, but how will I ever get there?" I discovered from Pisano that the training business was very lucrative, and a few years later I was invited to join David Sandler as one of his first franchised affiliates.

This gave me my first true mentor. Sandler was the best trainer I had ever seen, heard, or read. He was phenomenal at separating people from their money and he had truly mastered the art of training, as opposed to the teaching that so many other trainers did. On the other side of the coin, he was somewhat short sighted, often paranoid, and not really interested in long term coaching. As a trainer he had great material, he put on a great show, and he was extremely effective. Once the show was over, he had little interest in developing people. As for the other trainers like me, now under his wing, he inhibited growth instead of encouraging it, and this became the primary reason for our parting of the ways during 1990. I was determined to be the coach that he wasn't. I accomplished this by evaluating salespeople prior to training them.

Since Sandler didn't want to see me evaluating and training together, and this was clearly my intention, we went our separate ways. The weird part of this was the way I got in and out of business with him. By 1985 I had celebrated my ninth year in the music business and I hated it. The business I began in 1976 was fun, exciting, sometimes glamorous, and I was in love with it. The business I grew to hate was driven by product obsolescence, manufactures who didn't manufacture all that well, distributors who had difficulty distributing, sales reps who couldn't sell, and retailers who were clearly not in this business to make money. It was their hobby.

Just two days after my decision to leave the music business was made, I got a letter from David Sandler inviting me to hand him about $30 thousand dollars in return for some direction, his materials, some support, and his tutoring on becoming an effective trainer. It was another case of phenomenal timing as well as the universe playing its part in things just one more time. I seemed to be working in perfect harmony with the path I was destined to walk.

My expertise is clearly in sales, sales management, and training. I was managing and training salespeople as early as 1974. How I came to develop a computer software program is another example of strange but timely phenomenon. I became fascinated with computers when Texas Instruments introduced their little 99A4a home computer in the early eighties. I continued to play with a Kaypro portable and then on a Zenith laptop. It was with this Zenith laptop that the universe began to send me some very strong signals about what I was supposed to be doing.

Each night for nearly two years during 1986 and 1987 I sat with that computer, my imagination, some idea of what I wanted the screens to look like, a programming language I didn't have any hope of understanding, and no clue as to what I was doing. It was obvious after a few nights of almost trance-like-work what was taking place.

Several days earlier I went to a software store looking for a program to run my business. After failing to find any which would provide a data base, and handle accounts receivables with payment plans, and track multiple registrations for seminars, I knew I would have to get one custom written. At that time, early into a new business and in debt, I couldn't fathom spending $10 thousand dollars for customized software, and I had no idea that the help I was continuing to receive from the universe would extend to a sudden, overnight ability to do my own computer programming.

Each night I determined what I needed the software to do and each night my fingers, controlled by some more powerful source, would perfectly type in the correct code in a computer language which meant nothing to me at the time.

The finished program, one I continue to update to this very day, worked so well in the sales training business that copies of the application were sold to other sales trainers around the country. The real computing challenge was still to come.

In the summer of 1991 I decided to develop computer software which would help salespeople develop a sales plan from their goals, track their progress, and help them to book more strong appointments by phone. In concept it would be extremely powerful. The finished version was even better. My only question heading into the project was, "how much help would I get on this one?" Amazingly, I did this one on my own. I had learned enough along the way to actually become a bona fide computer programmer and PhoneSell was a real program, with real salespeople buying and using the application.

The universe even found a way to play a part in my sales training. From the earliest days I found myself being more a part of the audience than I was part of the actual training that I was doing. I heard myself engage in powerful dissertations not of my own conscious creation. Over and over I heard myself refer to Mindless Selling, before I even had an intellectual strong hold on its essence. So even this book was taking shape at some level, as far back as 1986 even though I had no idea that any of this was happening.

In 1988, while making entries in my dream book, I was moved to describe the woman of my dreams. I had not yet met Debbie, but I was able to describe her perfectly in my book. When we had our first date in August of the following year, I new from the first moment I saw her that she was in fact, the woman of my dreams, my soul mate, and it was love at first sight. But even here there was more to it than being able to marry the most wonderful woman in the world. Debbie is a marketing genius, and with her help, my small sales training business began to make the transition to a well known, well-respected firm of national prominence. While I now live up to my image, she created the image long before I was ready for it. Thanks to her dedication, creativity, unquestioning love, business expertise, inspiration, patience and impatience, my message is reaching companies, salespeople, executives and entrepreneurs nationally. Thank you Honey!

In 1991, while fighting for the right to run my evaluation business along with my training business I received a letter from the Massachusetts Department of Education. At first glance it looked devastating. It basically said that I couldn't continue to do business the way David Sandler had taught me to do business.

At about the tenth glance it was the "help" I needed. It not only provided me with the clean break I was in need of, but it also caused me to change the way I did business, with whom I did business, and for how much I would do business. The Universe came through and nudged me a little bit further down the path.

Dan Millman has been an inspiration to me as well. Although we have only met once and spoken by phone just twice, I feel as if he has personally mentored me. It was his first book, "The Way of the Peaceful Warrior", which I read in 1989. It helped me to get total control of my emotions, to stop worrying, and to stop trying to control the past and the future. Total control of the moment, in the moment. That's the Peaceful Warrior's way. Since Mindless Selling is very much dependent on one' ability to be in the moment I'm hoping that Dan won't have any objection to my use of the term "warrior" salesperson. I'd also highly recommend that you read at least two of his other books as well. "The Warrior Athlete" and "No Ordinary Moments" are books that you may find very helpful in making changes designed to give you control over your destiny.

When I spoke with Dan by phone in July of 1992 I told him of my plans for the book. He asked why I had waited so long and I told him of my frustrations with this project. I actually wanted to write the book in one sitting, but knew that it was not only unrealistic, but wouldn't provide the environment for quality work. That stopped me for a long time. In the true spirit of sales, I wanted a commitment from a publisher before I put pen to paper for the first time, but that wasn't all too realistic either, given the specialized readership of this book and my lack of literary skill.

Dan convinced me that the process in which this book would be written was what I still needed to learn to do in this lifetime. It would be a little at a time. And then some more. And then it would be rewritten, and rewritten again. There could have been no other way. Thank you Dan.

What I learned from all of these phenomena and the dozens of others not mentioned here is that the universe is always working in harmony with us, to help us, and even to reward us. I have witnessed the following scenario many times.

When a struggling salesperson finally writes his goals, commits to his sales plan and then faithfully executes the plan, he is often rewarded with much needed business literally dropping from the sky, straight down from the heavens and into his lap. Keep in mind that this new business isn't a result of his daily effort, because it's too early to see the fruits of a newly seeded garden. This business is a reward for finally putting forth the daily effort.

When you learn to recognize the messages and even the physical signals which are regularly being sent your way by sources more powerful than we can completely understand, we can work in complete harmony with the universe, gain cooperation from the universe, and ultimately reach all of our goals.

Richard Bandler, author of several books along with John Grinder, had an effect on my work. The two books which had the greatest influence were "Frogs Into Princes" and "Using Your Brain For a Change" Their work not only introduced me to NLP, a powerful reprogramming process which I learned to use on myself and others, but also to the magic behind creating long term bonding with total strangers in a matter of minutes.

Perhaps the greatest influences were the many small and large failures I endured all of which were responsible for producing wonderful lessons and of greater significance to my work, terrific stories. Robert Fulghum, author of such masterpieces as "All I

Needed to Know I Learned in Kindergarten", "It Was On Fire When I Lay Down On It", "Uh Oh", and "Maybe, Maybe Not" had a powerful effect on my ability to tell a story on the fly.

If there is one thing that will disarm a prospect in a pressure packed situation, it's a nice story about nice people who had similar problems, and who fought the appropriate solution in much the same way as the prospect who you are now with.

Collecting stories is good, but telling stories is better. Being a good storyteller is great. The ability to create a great story on the fly, using ingredients relevant to your immediate sales situation is art. Fulghum is an inspiration for that art.

MINDLESS SELLING-

THE 25 RULES

11

"Mindless selling is a way of life."

Dave Kurlan

Before I get specific about what mindless selling is, let me be very specific about what it isn't. If you ever find yourself thinking, creating, analyzing, strategizing, planning, worrying, anticipating, remembering, envisioning, fearing, anxious, panicking, excited, wondering, defending, explaining, uncomfortable, understanding, or fighting for survival on a sales call, then you are not practicing mindless selling. You are becoming emotionally involved, or simply talking to yourself. When you talk to yourself you listen to yourself as well, and not to your prospect. You may hear them speaking, but you can't effectively listen to them and listen for that which you need to hear. You're too busy. This causes you to lose objectivity, and when objectivity is lost, you lose control. When you lose control you'll often find yourself in a more intensive form of emotional involvement, often becoming defensive, or even explaining yourself. This is never powerful.

Mindless Selling is to be at peace.

Mindless selling is to be competetive.

Mindless selling is lucrative.

Mindless selling is rewarding.

Mindless selling is to have confidence.

Mindless selling is to have total control.

Mindless selling is to be fearless.

Mindless selling is to be rejection proof.

Mindless selling is to be a master.

Mindless selling is to be spontaneous.

Mindless selling as to be an actor.

Mindless selling is to be thought free.
Mindless selling is to have clear focus.
Mindless selling is to know people.
Mindless selling is to have momentary tolerance.
Mindless selling is a discipline.
Mindless selling is to be practiced daily.
Mindless selling requires a 100% commitment.
Mindless selling takes place in the moment.
Mindless selling is to be mentally tough.
Mindless selling requires keen listening skills.
Mindless selling is powerful.
Mindless selling requires that you trust yourself.
Mindless selling is a way of life.

"We sell peace, knowing that peace is the climate of freedom."

Dwight Eisenhower

Mindless Selling is to be at peace. You must be at total peace with yourself. Your life must be in order or, if it isn't, you can not bring it along with you. You must be free of all outside concerns. Total relaxation is required. If this is difficult for you then you may want to read Dr. Herbert Benson's book, "The Relaxation Response."

"Do not let what you can not do interfere with what you can do."

John Wooden

Mindless Selling is to be competitive. In this sense competition has very little to do with pricing and everything to do with competing to win. You are competing against your personal best performance each and every time you enter the "playing field."

"Business is never so healthy as when, like a chicken, it must do a certain amount of scratching for what it gets."

Henry Ford

Mindless Selling is lucrative. When the rules of Mindless Selling are applied in the daily sales arena, you will make substantially more money than a salesperson who merely goes out and does his job, often not to the very best of his ability.

"Every man of action has a strong dose of egoism, pride, hardness, and cunning. But all those things will be regarded as high qualities if he can make them the means to achieve great ends."

Unknown

Mindless Selling is rewarding. In addition to the money you will make and the recognition you will earn, you will be overtaken with deep feelings of satisfaction and pride in your work. Imagine being one of only a few people in the world who play professional sports, and the reverence their fans have toward them. Professional sales played mindlessly will bring similar rewards, recognition, and reverence.

"The most vital quality a soldier can possess is self confidence."

S. Gen. George Patton

Mindless Selling is to have confidence. It is always more powerful and more comforting to do something that you've already done successfully at least once before. The confidence gained from history helps you to achieve repeated successful outcomes.

"Believe in yourself! Have faith in your abilities. Without a humble but reasonable confidence in your own powers you can not be successful or happy."

Norman Vincent Peale

"When you have an elephant by the hind legs and he is trying to run away, it's best to let him run."

Abraham Lincoln

Mindless Selling is to have total control. Total control is the feeling you have when you always know, along each step of the way, exactly what will happen, and happen to you, next. When you have total control it will be possible to respond in the moment, and in a way which will help you to achieve your desired outcome.

"The only thing we have to fear is fear itself."

Franklin Delano Roosevelt

"It's not whether you get knocked down, it's whether you get up."

Vince Lombardi

Mindless Selling is to be fearless. Being afraid of a worst case scenario will inhibit you from making an appropriate "in the moment" response. As a matter of fact, fear takes you from the moment, causes you to become emotionally involved, and forces you to carefully choose your responses, rather than enabling you to respond spontaneously. Fearlessness keeps you in the moment, confident, and responding in a way which is appropriate for the situation. "When Smart People Fail", by Carol Hyatt is a good book for dealing with failure.

"Failure is only the opportunity to begin again more intelligently."

Henry Ford

Mindless Selling is to be rejection proof. Concern for being rejected is foolish because prospects do not reject people. They reject products, services, solutions, change, price, logistics, concepts, ideas, time wasters, games, and canned presentations and pitches. Cleansing your mind of these irrelevant matters will bring you back to the moment, empower you to be at your best, and help you to respond spontaneously.

"Excellence is to do a common thing in an uncommon way."
Booker T. Washington

Mindless Selling is being a master. George Leonard wrote a book called Mastery. Although the book is based on the principles of the martial arts, it is clearly a book that shows you how to master anything. Most salespeople have not even mastered the science portion of selling, not to mention the art, the music, or the mind. Mastery gives you ownership of the process and facilitates your ability to be in the moment.

"History is more or less bunk."
Henry Ford

Mindless Selling is to be spontaneous. It means that you won't have to think of an appropriate response, because the correct response, question, or statement will be generated as automatically as the next step you take climbing up a flight of stairs. You just decide which floor you wish to be on and then let your legs do the climbing.

"Am I not destroying my enemies when I make friends of them?"
Abraham Lincoln

Mindless Selling is being an actor. The beauty of acting is that you aren't playing yourself. You're playing the part of a highly successful salesperson that already has the characteristics; traits, skills, and mindset needed to employ mindless selling. When you play the part of this master repeatedly over time, you will become the master.

"I have not failed. I have (successfully) discovered 1200 materials that won't work.

Thomas Edison

"The heart of a fool is in his mouth, but the mouth of a wise man is in his heart."

Benjamin Franklin

Mindless Selling is to be thought free. Think of a time where you were so totally relaxed, so totally at peace, so totally stress and worry free, that you were truly able to "veg" out. There were no internal dialogues, no errands that you were supposed to run but didn't, no calls that needed to be made but weren't. No bills which had to be paid but weren't. You were totally free of thought. This is the mind that we need to develop in order to practice the art of mindless selling.

"If a man could have half of his wishes he would double his troubles."

Ben Franklin

Mindless Selling is having clear focus. Clear focus is knowing the exact details of desired outcome. You can clearly see the successful outcome and you never lose sight of that goal, be it a short range goal, like what you wish to accomplish at this meeting, or a long term goal, such as what you wish to accomplish in the next ten years. "Creative Visualization" by Shakti Gawain could be a great help to you in this area.

"Tact: the ability to describe others as they see themselves.
Abraham Lincoln

"The most important single ingredient in the formula for success is knowing how to get along with people."

Theodore Roosevelt

Mindless Selling is to know people. Knowing sales isn't enough. You must know people in much the same way that a machinist must know the machine he runs as well as he knows the procedure for making his particular part. A driver must know how his own car handles as well as he has learned the rules of the road. A salesperson must know people, and more specifically, the person he is selling to, as well or better than he knows the science and art of selling. Numerous books are available in the psychology section of your local bookstore. Some of my favorites are The Birth Order Book, by Dr. Kevin Leaman, Games People Play, by Dr. Eric Bierne, and I'm OK, Your OK", by Dr. Thomas Harris.

"I respect those who resist me but I can not tolerate them."

Charles DeGaulle

Mindless Selling is to have momentary tolerance. It is important to be tolerant of people's quirks, differences, ideas, philosophies, styles, and opinions. They are always right. There are no exceptions. Momentary tolerance is different from permanent tolerance in that you may only have to tolerate a prospect for the few minutes or hours you may be with him. If you were to tolerate or even buy into a sob story, excuse, lie, stall, or put off, you would take that home with you. Cause and effect result in a permanent tolerance of their put off, and you will own it at some significant cost to you.

"Your chances of doing business today are in direct proportion to the patience you show today."

Dave Kurlan

"Patience means self-suffering."

Mahatma Ghandi

Mindless Selling is to have momentary patience. The more important that it is to do business with someone today, or the more you want to close the business today, the important it is that you be patient with your prospect.

".... Have five minutes more patience than your opponent, and you will always be the victor."

Nicolas Risini

Mindless Selling is a discipline. It must be a practice put to regular use. You must apply it on easy prospects and difficult ones alike. It is a full time proposition, not to be applied only when you feel like it, rather, to be applied each and every moment of the sales day.

"Winning is a habit. Unfortunately, so is losing."

Vince Lombardi

Mindless Selling must be practiced. To master mindless selling you must devote at least thirty minutes to practice each day. Work especially hard on these scenarios which cause you the most difficulty. These situations should be role played until you can respond, rather than react, in the moment.

"Don't be humble. You're not that great."

Golda Meir

Mindless Selling requires a 100% commitment. You must be committed to the process, to being the best that you can be, and to doing whatever it takes. Do whatever it takes to become the best and whatever it takes to change. Do whatever it takes to win, and whatever it takes each and every day with each and every prospect.

"The quality of a person's life is in direct proportion to their commitment to excellence."

Vince Lombardi

Mindless Selling takes place in the moment. When you aren't playing "what if" with your future and you're not fretting over the "if onlys" of your past, you can be in the moment. When your mind is thought free and you're not emotionally involved, you can be in the moment. When you're relaxed and unhurried you can be in the moment. When you fully trust your own ability you can be in the moment. When you arm wrestle life by attempting to control your past or your future, you'll have no control over "right now." Consistent lack of control over right now, over time, gives you no control over anything. Consistent control over right now, this moment, over time, gives you total control of your future.

"I never think of the future. It comes soon enough."

Albert Einstein

Mindless Selling is to be mentally tough. The bad days will take their toll and the tough prospects will weaken you. With a mentally tough attitude, one that appears harmless on the surface, but one that says, "I am in total control of the way I feel, and I feel strong", no one can get to you. Killer instinct. Make sure that no one slips through your fingers. Make sure that you let no one off the hook.

"Nothing great will ever be achieved without great men, and men are great only if they are determined to be so."

Charles DeGaulle

Mindless Selling requires keen listening skills. Everyone reminds you that good salespeople ask good questions but until you have exceptional listening skills, you won't really ask the right questions. Sharpen your listening skills and your power of observation by playing the game Merlin. Become a kid in a candy store, in awe of everything, especially those things you presume to know. The best questions to ask are the ones to which you think you know the answers.

"Silence is the ultimate weapon of power."

Charles DeGaulle

"The most rewarding of all talents is that of never using two words when one will do."

Thomas Jefferson

Mindless Selling is powerful. You won't believe how much true power you have over the spoken word, your thoughts, your emotions, and especially over your prospects when you are selling mindlessly. Power is money.

"Being powerful is like being a lady. If you have to tell people you are, you aren't."

Margaret Thatcher

Mindless Selling is to have trust in your own ability. You must trust yourself to do the right thing, have total faith in your ability, trust your judgment, and confidence that the words which are uttered by you, in the moment, without censorship, will not only flow from your lips and roll off of your tongue, but be the right words as well.

"Self-trust is the first secret of success"

Ralph Waldo Emerson

"The world cares very little about what a man or woman knows; it is what the man or woman does that counts."

Booker T. Washington

Mindless Selling is a way of life. You will find yourself preaching the mindless way to friends and colleagues. Peers will approach you in total amazement of your ability to stay so cool, appear so non threatening, look so flexible, remain so tough, and to always have the right move to make, at the right time, with the right consequences, and make it all look so easy. This will flow into every day life and become a part of you, strengthen your communication skills, your relationships, and your passion for life. At first, mindless selling is like free falling from an airplane 5,000 feet above the ground. You know it's happening, but you don't know how it's gonna end up. Mastered, it's as mindless as going to the bathroom upon waking - you just do it- and as invigorating as making love.

"Old age is like a plane flying through a storm. Once you're aboard there's nothing you can do."

Golda Meir

"Life is a series of moments. To live each one is to succeed."

Corita Kent

Speaking of making love, please avoid premature presentation. This takes place when you can't wait long enough to give your solution to the prospect. Instead of saving the best for last, when you know everything is ready, in place, and appropriate, you climax too early, resulting in a very unrewarding call. So mind the four play of selling as well. Get your prospect hot before you climax!

"Successful salesman: Someone who has found a cure for the common cold shoulder."

Robert Olson

BIBLIOGRAPHY

All I Ever Needed to Know I Learned in Kindergarten
Robert Fulghum, Random House

The Birth Order Book
Dr. Kevin Leamen, Dell

Confessions of an S.O.B.
Al Neuhearth,

Frogs Into Princes
Richard Bandler and John Grinder, Real People Press

Games People Play
Dr. Eric Bierne, Random House

I'll See It When I Believe It
Dr. Wayne Dyer, Avon

It Was On Fire When I Lay Down On It
Robert Fulghum, Random House

Mastery
George Leonard, Plume

No Ordinary Moments
Dan Millman, JH Kramer

I'm OK, Your'e OK
Dr. Thomas Harris, Avon

The Relaxation Response
Dr. Herbert Benson, Avon

The Warrior Athlete
Dan Millman, JH Kramer

Using Your Brain For a Change
Richard Bandler and John Grinder, Real People Press

Uh-Oh
Robert Fulghum, Random House

I

Way of the Peaceful Warrior

Dan Millman, Stillpoint

Your Erroneous Zones

Dr. Wayne Dyer, Avon

ABOUT THE AUTHOR

Dave Kurlan is the president of David Kurlan & Associates and a principal of The Objective Management Group, international sales management consulting firms, both with headquarters in Massachusetts. He possesses 25 years of experience in all facets of sales training, sales management and consulting.

A regularly featured Conference attraction, Dave has been a top rated speaker at **Inc.** *Magazine's Conference on Growing the Company* since 1991, was featured at the *Sales & Marketing Management Conference* in 1996 and will be featured at *DCI's* four national *Sales Management Conferences* in 1997. Nationally known for his ground breaking work in evaluating sales people, he is the developer of *The Dave Kurlan Sales Force Profile*, an evaluation tool, a unique audio CD sales training library called *Unreal Sales Calls* and co-developer of *Salesmind,* computer software that helps salespeople overcome their self-limiting weaknesses, and.

He has written a regular monthly column on selling for *The Electrical Distributor Magazine* and has been featured on radio, television and in print. Dave has been featured in Inc. Magazine, Selling Power, Sales & Marketing Management Magazine and Incentive Magazine. He has written a book on sales called *Mindless Selling*, and a sales manual called *Orchestrating The Sale.* He is featured on Inc. Magazine's video *How to Increase Sales and Profits by 1000%* and specializes in working with growing companies.